Creating
Crystal Jewelry
with Swarovski

65 Sparkling Designs with Crystal Beads and Stones

Laura McCabe

Creative Publishing
international

Creative Publishing
international

Copyright © 2008 Laura McCabe

Creative Publishing international, Inc.

400 First Avenue North

Minneapolis, MN 55401

1-800-328-3895

www.creativepub.com

ISBN-13: 978-1-58923-345-4

ISBN-10: 1-58923-345-X

10 9 8 7 6 5 4 3 2

Library of Congress Cataloging-in-Publication Data

McCabe, Laura.

  Creating crystal jewelry with Swarovski : 65 sparkling designs with crystal beads and stones / Laura McCabe.

     p. cm.

  ISBN 1-58923-345-X

  1. Beadwork--Patterns. 2. Jewelry making. 3. Swarovski (Firm) I. Title.

TT860.M37 2008

745.594'2--dc22   2007034367

                                                                    CIP

Technical Editor: Judith Durant

Project Manager: Amy C. Fletcher

Copy Editor: Kristy Mulkern

Proofreader: Elizabeth Foz

Book Design: Stephen Gleason

Cover Design: Stephen Gleason

Page Layout: Stephen Gleason

Illustrations: Julia S. Pretl

Photographs: Jack Deutsch Photography

Photo Stylist: Laura Maffeo

Printed at R.R. Donnelley

*D*uring the past few years, I have focused my efforts almost entirely on making bead-woven jewelry with crystal beads and stones. Inspired by a love of historical costume, an appreciation of anything vintage, and an obsession with all things sparkly, I have worked to incorporate not only beads into my work, but also some of the fabulous crystal stones found in costume jewelry. I have a much more simple taste in the jewelry I choose to wear, but the opportunity to design and create with endless "bling" has brought me much pleasure and a real appreciation for crystal as an object. I hope these projects will inspire each of you to continue along a path of creativity, originality, and craftsmanship that celebrates the past and, with our dedication, will persevere for generations into the future.

Thanks to all the people without whose dedication, hard work, and patience this book would not have been possible.

First and foremost, thanks to my husband, Michael, who has been my greatest advocate, an endless source of support and encouragement, and the one to organize me enough to make this book happen.

Thank you to my family and friends whose encouragement, support, and patience have carried me through the past few years, and thanks to Po, for her company and presence in the writing of this book.

Thanks to all my students, who over the years have helped to refine these projects. Thanks to Deborah Cannarella, editorial mastermind and general overseer. Thanks to project manager Amy Fletcher and art director Sylvia McArdle. Thanks also to Jack Deutsch and Laura Maffeo, photographer and stylist, whose efforts exceeded all my wildest expectations and successfully captured the intricacy and detail of beadwork. Thanks also to Julia Pretl, graphic illustrator extraordinaire; to Judith Durant, technical editor; and to all the other folks at Rockport Publishers and Creative Publishing international for their labors and efforts.

This book is dedicated to the woman who kept me laughing when I probably should have been crying. For your endless support, wisdom and humor, thank you Lilli B.

Crystal Flat-Back Flower Brooch, page 11

CONTENTS

6

Chapter One
The Fashion History of Cut Crystal

Cut crystal has a fascinating history, in which crystal objects are intertwined with beauty, aristocracy, costume history, and couture fashion. First developed in the eighteenth century in English glassworks, cut crystal (a leaded glass) was intended to capture the luxury and opulence of aristocratic costume and jewelry. During this time, Georges-Frederic Strass, jeweler to the French king Louis XV, set cut crystals in ornate settings as if they were gemstones. For the next few centuries, the name "Strass" was tied to the concept of crystal jewelry—and was, in fact, another name for cut stones.

In the late-nineteenth century, when the glass industry of Europe was in Bohemia, jewelry and cut-crystal design were influenced by the elaborate beauty of the Byzantine and Austro-Hungarian empires. In this golden age of industrialism and unmatched aesthetics, cut crystal made a giant leap forward, thanks to a young, entrepreneurial artisan named Daniel Swarovski.

After apprenticing to crystal cutters in Bohemia and developing his own mechanized crystal-cutting technology, Swarovski moved to Wattens, a small village in Austria. In 1895, he founded the Swarovski company with two partners, Franz Weis and Armand Kosmann. A few years later, the Swarovski family took sole ownership of the company, which is still a family-owned business.

Throughout the twentieth century, the Swarovski name and the product it represents were inextricably tied to haute couture and the fashion industry. Great designers of the modern era worked directly with the Swarovski company. Coco Chanel, Elsa Schiaparelli, Paul Poiret, Madame Vionnet, and Christian Dior—to name a few —all worked with Swarovski's stones and beads to add the magic of crystal to their designs. In the early 1950s, Dior worked closely with Manfed Swarovski to create the now well-known AB, or Aurora Borealis, finish.

Crystal found its way into every walk of life from the glamorous fashions of Hollywood in the 1930s and 1940s to the funkadelic, futuristic groove of garments of the 1960s. The quality, elegance, and sparkle appeal of crystal have made it a timeless fashion statement.

Today, the magic and beauty of crystal still capture our imagination. It embellishes couture and ready-to-wear fashions and is a popular trend in the DIY (do it yourself) world. The Swarovski company, now in its fifth generation, still produces high-quality beads and stones that, with cutting-edge technology, will continue to sparkle long into the future.

Chapter Two
Seed Beads and Crystals

*Y*ou can buy seed beads in a wide range of sizes from a number of sources. These beads are made today as they always have been —a long tube of glass is drawn across a wooden or metal support that runs the length of a large room. When the glass tube hardens, it is cut into small pieces. The pieces are then tumbled to smooth the edges and make the seed beads.

Seed Beads

Historically, seed beads were made primarily in Europe. With their strong focus on glassmaking, Italy, the former Czechoslovakia (now the Czech Republic and Slovakia), and France have traditionally been the primary producers of seed beads. Since the 1950s, the technologically advanced Japanese have come onto the market with a more perfect, more consistent bead. Today, some people consider the Japanese beads superior to European beads because of this consistency in shape and size and the fact that they also have a larger hole size.

Traditionally, seed-bead sizing was determined by how many beads fit into a linear inch. With modern technology, however, the beads are now smaller and don't conform to the old standards. Although there is a wide range of sizes in seed beads, from 2° to 24°, the projects in this book require three basic sizes: 11°, 12°, and 15°. These sizes are, by far, the most common sizes for woven beadwork. As with needles, bead size decreases as the number increases—for example, a 15° bead is smaller than an 11°.

Seed beads

Japanese Cylinder Beads

These cylindrical beads are available in several sizes, the most essential being 11°. They differ from other beads in that they have a tubular, rather than spherical, shape. Due to their shape, they fit together like tiles, and work well for bezeling and peyote stitch. The end result is a neater, more polished look than the look that can be achieved with round seed beads.

Japanese cylinder beads are marketed under several trademarked names, including Delicas (Miyuki Company), Treasures (Toho Company), and Aikos (Toho Company's high-precision cylinder beads).

Three-cuts

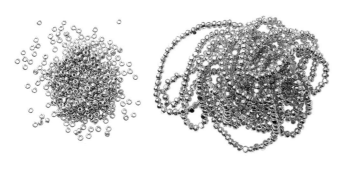

Charlottes

Japanese 12° Three-cuts and 15° Three-cuts

After they have been tumbled and retumbled to smooth the sharp edges, these seed beads are cut with three facets. The facets create a sparkling effect and add a vintage look to the finished work. Generally, a 12° is an adequate substitute for an 11° seed bead (Japanese three-cut beads are not made in 11°). The 15° three-cut works well in place of the 15° round.

Czech 15° Charlottes

Many of the projects in this book call for 15° Czech charlottes. These small seed beads, produced in the Czech Republic, have a single facet. Although they are labeled 15°, they are actually considerably smaller than Japanese 15's and are excellent for the type of bezeling featured in chapter five.

Crystal Beads

Here you will find a description of each of the types and sizes of crystal beads you'll need for the projects in this book. For easy reference, I have also provided the Swarovski article numbers. These numbers are exclusively Swarovski numbers and are not used by other crystal producers. I have also included the Swarovski article number in the materials box for each project to make it easier for you to find the materials you need.

Bicones
(Swarovski article #5301)

Bicones are crystal beads with two cones, drilled point to point, to form a bicone shape. These crystals are faceted and available in a wide range of sizes. For the projects in this book, you will work with 3mm and 4mm bicone beads.

Faceted rounds
(Swarovski article #5000)

These beads are faceted, center-drilled, round beads. They are available in a wide range of sizes. For the projects in this book, you will work with 2mm, 3mm, and 4mm faceted rounds.

Faceted rondelles
(Swarovski article #5040)

These rondelles are doughnut-shaped, center-drilled, multifaceted beads. They come in a wide range of sizes, starting at 6mm. For the projects in this book, you will need 6mm and 8mm rondelles.

Margaritas
(Swarovski article #3700)

Margaritas are flat, flower-shaped beads that are drilled through at the center of the flower. They are available in a wide range of sizes. For the projects in this book, you will need 6mm and 10mm margaritas.

Lentil beads
(Swarovski article #335)

True to its name, this vintage bead has a multifaceted, lentil shape. Lentil beads are available in a wide variety of sizes. They are featured in the Rings & Things Necklaces on pages 90–95.

Crystal Stones

Although traditionally most often used in costume jewelry, crystal stones are a great addition to woven beadwork. They come in a wide range of sizes, shapes, and colors.

Rivolis
(Swarovski article #1122)

The rivoli is a classic crystal stone shape. This 32-faced, round stone is pointed on the front and back sides. Rivolis are available in foiled (with enamel backing) and nonfoiled (clear) styles, in many sizes. The projects in this book require 10, 12, 14, 16, and 18mm rivolis.

Dentelles
(Swarovski vintage article #1200)

The dentelle is another classic crystal stone shape, but, unfortunately, is no longer being made in larger sizes. You can only buy these larger vintage pieces online or in specialized bead shops. The dentelle is a round stone with 17 front facets and 16 back facets, forming a multi-faceted, flat-topped stone with a sharply pointed back. Like rivolis, this stone may be foiled or nonfoiled. It is sized with the designation "ss" (stone size). (See page 143 for a stone size to millimeter conversion chart.)

For the projects in this book, you will need 55ss, 60ss, and 65ss dentelles. If you can't find this vintage stone, substitute an equivalent-sized rivoli or other round crystal stone.

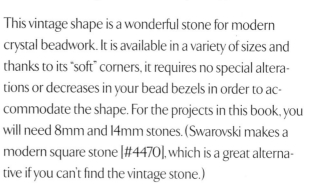

Crystal frames
(Swarovski article #4439)

This modern crystal shape looks like a sparkling picture frame. It comes in a variety of sizes and colors and makes an excellent component piece. For the projects in this book, you will need 14mm frames.

Crystal rings
(Swarovski article #1245)

Another modern crystal shape, these faceted crystal rings are available in a variety of colors, but in only one size: 13mm. As with the crystal frames, they make a spectacular component piece.

Large crystal stones, 27mm
(Swarovski article #1201)

Another classic stone shape, still in production, is the 27mm round stone. With its 33 facets and shallow profile, it makes a stunning centerpiece on any type of beaded crystal jewelry. This stone is also available foiled or nonfoiled and in a range of colors. In addition to the 27mm size, this stone (#1201) is also available in a vintage 17mm size, which makes a great substitute for the rivolis in some of the projects in this book.

Square rivolis
(Swarovski vintage article #4650)

This vintage shape is a wonderful stone for modern crystal beadwork. It is available in a variety of sizes and thanks to its "soft" corners, it requires no special alterations or decreases in your bead bezels in order to accommodate the shape. For the projects in this book, you will need 8mm and 14mm stones. (Swarovski makes a modern square stone [#4470], which is a great alternative if you can't find the vintage stone.)

Chapter Three
Tools and Materials

*I*n beadwork, there is a distinct advantage when it comes to tools. Bead weaving—and the various other techniques needed for the projects in this book—requires a very limited number of inexpensive and readily available tools and materials. So, this type of work is accessible to just about everyone and is very portable, too. Here's what you'll need to have in your toolbox.

A FireLine

B Microcrystalline Wax

C No-Tangle Bobbins

D One-G Nylon Thread

E Nymo Nylon Thread

F English Beading and English Glover's Needles

Scissors

Be sure to have a good pair of sharp embroidery scissors. You'll need these to cut thread ends close to the finished work without leaving small tails. If you are going to be working with leather or fabric, you'll also need a pair of sewing shears.

When working with FireLine thread (a braided wire), you will need a third pair. I recommend children's Fiskars, which are inexpensive, easy to find, and relatively small. FireLine will quickly dull any pair of scissors, and you are better off with an inexpensive, disposable pair rather than sacrificing those fine embroidery scissors.

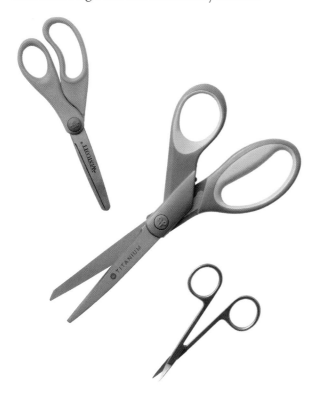

English Beading Needles
(sizes 10, 12, 13, and 15)

Although there is a wide range of needle types out there, I generally prefer to work with English needles. They are slightly thinner in size and tend to hold up better to handling than some other types of needles. They come in a variety of sizes, ranging from size 10 to size 15 (the larger the number, the thinner the needle). It is generally a good idea to have some of every size in your toolbox. Size 12 is a great, all-purpose size, although some projects may require a thinner or thicker needle. Check the materials box included with each project.

English Glover's Needles
(sizes 10 and 12)

Keep a few glover's needles on hand. Traditionally, glove makers and leatherworkers used these needles, and they're great for bead embroidery on leather. Just as with beading needles, a larger number correlates with a thinner needle. A size 10 glover's needle will fit through an 11° seed bead. A size 12 glover's needle will fit through a 15° seed bead. Because these leather needles have a barbed, triangular tip, they can be quite sharp. Be careful when working with them.

Microcrystalline Wax

There are various types of thread conditioners on the market. My own preference is for microcrystalline wax (a synthetic, nonorganic wax). This wax is usually sold in small plastic tubs and often labeled as "synthetic beeswax." Unlike real beeswax, it does not get rancid over time and does not dry out in cold or dry climates, but remains sticky.

No-Tangle Bobbins

No doubt. In bead weaving, "thread management" can be a serious issue. To help combat this problem, you may want to have some of these small, plastic, fold-up bobbins on hand. These are great for winding up threads when you are not working with them. They are also perfect for packing up your beadwork to ensure safe, no-tangle transport.

FireLine

(fishing line/beading thread)

The projects in this book are made with FireLine, a round, braided, plastic-coated metal fishing wire produced by Berkley for sport fishing. Not only is it great for fishing, it is a thread for crystal beading. It's strong and won't split or fray the way that nylon threads do.

FireLine is available in a wide range of sizes, but for this type of beadwork, 6 lb. or 4 lb. test works best. It is also available in a few different colors. Generally, the crystal color (actually more white than clear) is great for light-to-midrange bead colors. Smoke (a grayish black) is better when working with dark-colored beads.

Flatten the end of the strand with your fingernails or pliers to make it easier to thread the needle. Lightly coat the strand with microcrystalline wax by running it through the wax. This will keep the kinks out of the thread as you work and will improve tension on the otherwise slick surface.

Nylon Thread

Many companies make nylon thread, which comes in a range of colors, so it's easy to match the colors of your project. I don't use nylon thread for woven work, but I do use it when I need to sew on a leather backing—as for the Crystal Flat-Back Flower Brooch (page 110). I generally use a D-weight thread, which is quite durable, yet fits easily through any size seed bead. Keep in mind that, although nylon thread is great for leather and seed-bead stitch work, it does not hold up well to the sharp edges of crystal beads and crystal stones. Nymo is one of the most popular brands of nylon monofilament thread for beadwork, but newer brands have come onto the market, such as One-G and C-Ion.

Leather or Ultrasuede

You will also need leather for any of the projects that have embroidery or embroidered bezels for stones. If you work with leather, make sure you are working with very soft, supple, garment-grade split hide. The leather should be soft enough that you can sew through it even with a beading needle—although you can always switch to a glover's needle if you are having trouble. A great alternative to leather is Ultrasuede, a washable suedelike synthetic available at most fabric shops.

Thread Burner

Although not absolutely necessary, a thread burner can be a handy tool. Originally used for medical cauterization, these battery-powered burners are great for getting rid of any tiny tails or thread fuzz left on the finished work.

Beading Board

It's essential to have a good work surface. There are many surfaces available, including soft Vellux blanket squares, velvet bead boards, and plastic trays. Most surfaces have a velvety texture to keep the beads from rolling around.

My preference is for the 14" by 7 ¾" (35.6 × 19.7 cm) velvet boards, traditionally used for jewelry display. They come in a wide range of colors and make it easy to move your work to other locations without having to pick up all the beads you've laid out. If you put the boards in the display trays made to fit them, they are stackable and have an edge that keeps the beads from rolling off.

Chain-nose Pliers

Although chain-nose pliers are not a traditional beading tool, they are great for breaking out extra beads or pulling on needles when you need a little extra leverage. These pliers are available in a range of prices, from the high-end, German pliers to inexpensive imports. (If you work with with silver you may want to opt for the top of the line; otherwise, keep it simple and keep it cheap.)

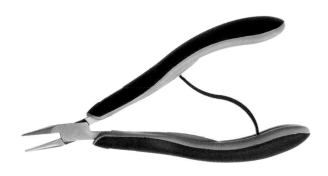

Task Lamp

Good lighting is essential when doing beadwork, both by day and by night. Because tungsten lights are not particularly bright and also distort color, be sure to have a full spectrum or "daylight" bulb lamp. There are many types on the market, including the OTT-Lite and Daylight brands. If you do a lot of beading away from home, get one of the portable versions of these lamps. Most classrooms for workshops will have accessible outlets for your light, although you may want to carry an extension cord with you just in case.

Measuring Tape

A measuring tape or ruler is always great to have on hand. You will need one when sizing finished work or when fitting the intended jewelry wearer.

E6000 Adhesive

When applying cabochons or flat-backs to leather, E6000 is my adhesive of choice. It is strong, quick drying, and removable, which is handy if I happen to put it in the wrong place. It is also very fumy, so use it only in a well-ventilated area and avoid inhaling the fumes. For those who have trouble working with chemical adhesives, the alternative is double-sided carpet tape, which is available at most craft and hardware stores.

Chapter Four
Four Basic Stitches

Off-loom beadwork incorporates a large variety of stitches that originate from many different cultures and regions. Beadwork is one of the many universal human endeavors that link people throughout time and across cultures. By working with these multiple techniques, we are collaborating, so to speak, with the people of these cultures to satisfy one of our most instinctive desires: to create beautiful personal adornment.

For the projects in this book, you will work with four basic beading stitches. If you need to, refer back to these instructions as you work through the techniques and projects.

Stitch 1: Basic Bead Embroidery

Next to stringing, embroidery is probably the most ancient beading technique. For centuries, humans have used beads to adorn their clothing and personal belongings. Today, many garments are made and worn with elaborate surface bead embroidery.

While there are a couple of different forms of bead embroidery, I use a technique that I call "basic beaded backstitch embroidery," using a basic sewing backstitch to apply beads of any size and shape to any sort of textile surface. Usually I use leather or Ultrasuede as my textile surface, but this technique can be used on fabrics of all sorts.

1. To begin, thread a needle with the desired length of single beading thread. Tie a knot to keep the thread from coming all the way through the textile.

2. Coming up through the textile surface, pick up six seed beads (of the desired size), lay them flat against the textile, and go back down through the surface right after the sixth bead. Now, on the underside of the textile surface, go back and come up between the third and fourth bead in the sequence of six **(a)**. Travel through beads 4, 5, and 6 again, and now you are ready to add six new beads and repeat the process again and again.

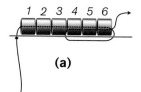

(a)

Tip: Knotting

Here's a great knot for bead embroidery. Form a slip knot with the tail of your thread. Then pass the tail through the loop and pull it to tighten the knot. This knot is large enough so that it won't pull through the textile when you take the first stitch.

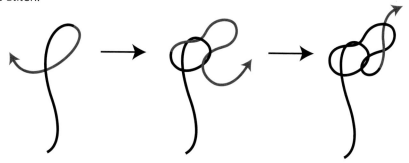

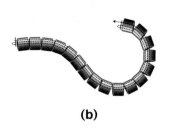

(b)

Although you can always use fewer than six beads each time, six beads is about the maximum number you can use without the fabric buckling. This technique can be used to embroider straight lines, curls, curves, and any sort of line drawing.

After you have secured your initial rows, go back and pass through the beads a second, third, and even fourth time with your thread to help stabilize and neaten the rows **(b)**.

Stitch 2: Basic Peyote Stitch

Peyote stitch has its origins in Native American and ancient Egyptian cultures, among others. This highly versatile stitch creates a fabric made entirely of beads. It can be woven in both flat and tubular form, with an even or odd number of beads in each row. For these projects, you will work flat even-count, flat odd-count, and tubular even-count stitches.

FLAT EVEN-COUNT PEYOTE STITCH

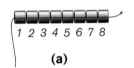

1 2 3 4 5 6 7 8

(a)

1. To create a piece of flat even-count peyote stitch, string a number of beads to make the desired width of the finished piece, tab, strip, etc. The number may be any even number from two beads to hundreds of beads, depending on the scale of your work. The illustration shows eight beads **(a)**.

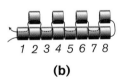

1 2 3 4 5 6 7 8

(b)

2. After you pick up the correct number of beads, pick up another bead, and go back through the second-to-last bead in the initial row (#7) in the opposite direction. Now pick up a new bead, skip over the next bead in the work (#6), and go through the bead after that (#5). Work in this manner until you reach the other side, where you first began. A row of peyote stitch consists of "every other bead," so after you have added this row, the initial strand of eight has split into two rows, for a total of three rows (if you count the most recent) **(b)**.

3. You are now ready to work back in the other direction and make another row, putting a bead in every "low spot" **(c)**. Continue working back and forth in this manner to desired length. Because every other bead constitutes a bead in that row, peyote stitch is always counted on the diagonal.

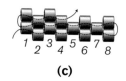

(c)

FLAT ODD-COUNT PEYOTE STITCH

Flat odd-count peyote stitch is somewhat more difficult than even count. It requires a series of U-turns within the work to accommodate the extra column of beads.

1. To begin, pick up the number of beads to make the desired width of the finished piece, tab, strip, etc. This number can be any odd number from three beads to hundreds of beads, depending on the scale of your work. The illustration shows nine beads **(d)**.

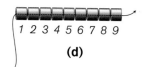

(d)

2. Once you pick up the correct number of beads, pick up another bead and go back through the second-to-last bead in the initial row (#8) in the opposite direction. Now pick up a new bead, skip over the next bead, and go through the bead after that. Work in this manner until you reach the other side, where you first began **(e)**. As with the even-count peyote, the addition of this row will split the first strand of nine beads into two rows of peyote stitch.

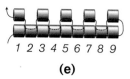

(e)

Tip: Counting Rows

One way to count rows in flat peyote stitch is to hold your woven piece on its side and count the number of beads up that side. Then flip it over and count the number of beads up the other side. Add these two numbers together and you have the row count.

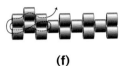

(f)

3. What makes odd-count peyote different is that there is not a bead to go through at the end of the row. Some manipulation is required to make the stitch work properly. When you've picked up a bead at the end of a row, go back through the bead below the one you just picked up. Now weave back through three of the beads within the piece, doing a U-turn so you come back in the opposite direction. At the edge, do one more U-turn, and you will come out of the last bead added in the opposite direction, ready to peyote-stitch the next row **(f)**.

One side always has a straightforward turn. The other side will require this series of back tracks and U-turns in order to position the thread properly for the next row.

TUBULAR EVEN-COUNT PEYOTE STITCH

Although there is both a tubular even- and odd-count peyote stitch, you will only need to know the even-count version for the projects in this book. Tubular even-count peyote is perfect for bezeling stones and making various ring shapes.

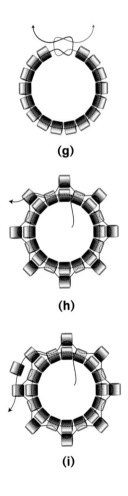

(g)

(h)

(i)

1. To begin, string an even number of beads on a single-threaded needle. Slide the beads down, leaving a tail. Tie a square knot to form a circle of beads **(g)**.

2. Go through a couple of beads to hide the knot, then, coming out of a bead in the circle, pick up a new bead, skip over the next bead, and go through the bead after that **(h)**.

3. After you have gotten all the way round the circle, you will need to do a "step up." A step up is a thread pass that will bring your working thread up to the next row in order to continue weaving. It's easy to remember the step up because at the end of each row, you will have to pass through two beads (the last one in the row you are working around and the first one in the row you have just laid down) in order to begin another row **(i)**.

Stitch 3: Basic Spiral Rope

This spiral stitch is derived from South African beadwork, most likely of the Zulu tribe, known for its elaborate and ornate tubular beadwork. It is a great multipurpose stitch that makes an excellent pendant chain and also a flexible and strong base for embellishments and bead weaving. There are many variations of spiral rope—the most basic form, shown here, is made with two colors of 11° Japanese seed beads. There are crystal variations of this stitch in some of the projects. One color seed bead will be the inside or core color (CC) of the rope. The other color will be the outside color (OC) of the rope. You will need three times as much of the outside color as the core color.

1. Begin by single-threading about two wingspans of Fire-Line and wax the thread well. (A wingspan is a length as long as your open arms, approximately 5 feet [1.5 m].) Spiral is a very "thread hungry" stitch, so you will need to begin a new thread several times during the course of making a necklace base.

2. Thread four CC beads and three OC beads. Be sure to leave at least a 14" (35.6 cm) tail at the end of the thread. Pass back through the four CC beads, creating a circle. Hold this base circle in your hand with the OC beads on the left **(a)**.

(a)

Tip: Working with Long Threads

Spiral rope and tubular Ndebele work the same from either direction, so you can work with long threads to avoid lots of thread add-ons. Begin with a long section of thread and wind half of it onto a bobbin. When you have worked the rope or spiral on that thread, unwind the bobbin, thread the needle, and work in the opposite direction. It's also easier to work with only half the thread length.

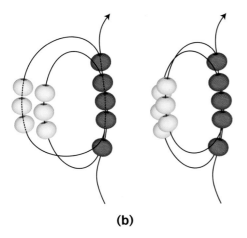

(b)

3. Next, pick up one CC and three OC beads. Slide all the beads down to the base. Circle around and pass through the four previous CC beads (including the one you just added). Flip the last stitch over to the left. Continue to repeat this pattern, and a spiral cord will begin to form. You will probably have to tie off and start a new thread at least once while making this spiral rope base. Be sure to knot off in the outer beads, not the core beads, as you may want to work embellishments off the core beads later **(b)**.

Stitch 4: Ndebele or Herringbone

Ndebele stitch, or herringbone stitch, originates with the Ndebele tribe of South Africa. It has both flat and tubular forms, but you will only need to know tubular Ndebele for the projects in this book. Tubular Ndebele consists of a sequence of ladders around the perimeter of the tube. Each ladder is two beads wide. The beads are positioned next to each other at an angle to create a herringbone pattern.

There are several ways to begin tubular Ndebele. This method is the traditional way to begin—and also preferable because it can be worked the same from either end, allowing you to seamlessly join two separate tubes.

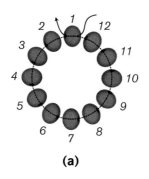

(a)

1. The number of ladders around the tube determines the number of beads you pick up to begin. For every ladder, you will need to pick up four beads. In the example shown here, the tube will have three ladders. So, you begin by stringing twelve beads (three ladders x four beads per ladder = twelve). When you have strung your initial count of beads, go back through the first bead to form a circle **(a)**. Do not tie a knot.

2. As shown in the drawing, pick up two new beads and go through the very next bead (#2). Then skip over the next two beads (#3 and #4) in the circle and go through the bead after that (#5). Now pick up two new beads and go through the very next bead (#6). Then skip over two beads (#7 and #8) in the circle and go through the bead after that (#9). Pick up two new beads and go into the very next bead (#10). Then skip over the next two beads in the circle (#11 and #12) and go through the next bead (#1). At this point, you will need to step up through the first bead added. Then you are ready to begin tubular Ndebele **(b)**.

This traditional start can be a little tricky when you first learn it, but the benefits far outweigh the disadvantages. When you pull on your thread, the beads should shift into place and form the three ladders. You may need to fiddle to get the ladders in the correct position to start stitching **(c)**.

3. After the base is formed, every subsequent row is the same. Coming out of one of the beads in the first ladder, pick up two beads and go down into the second bead in that ladder. Do a U-turn and come out the next bead in the next ladder as shown in the drawing. Pick up two beads, and go back down the second bead in this second ladder **(d)**. The drawing shows tubular Ndebele blown out into a 2D illustration.

4. Continue all the way around until you get back to the first ladder. Just as in tubular even-count peyote, you will have a step up at the end of each row **(e)**. If you forget the step-up, your tubular Ndebele ladders will start spiraling rather than continuing straight.

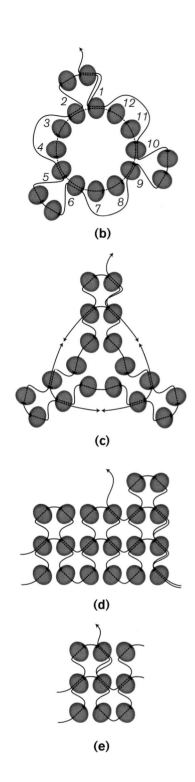

(b)

(c)

(d)

(e)

Chapter Five

Two Bezeling Techniques

The technique of enclosing or "capturing" a stone is called bezeling. Bezeling is a technique familiar to metalsmiths, and beadworkers have adapted it to form settings in woven beadwork. Cabochons and crystal stones have no holes in them, so you need to create bezels to hold the stones in place.

There are two basic techniques for bezeling stones. The first involves attaching the stone to a leather or fabric surface and bezeling it while it is on that surface. This technique is excellent when working with flat-backed cabochons and stones. The second technique involves bezeling the stone with an open-back bezel. This method is best for bezeling point-backed stones, such as rivolis and dentelles, which cannot be attached directly to a flat surface.

Technique 1: Stones Bezeled onto a Surface

This method works well for bezeling any flat-backed cabochon or crystal to a fabric or leather surface. The directions call for E6000 adhesive, but if you find the fumes too strong, work with double-sided tape instead. Simply place a small piece of tape wherever the directions call for adhesive.

1. With a toothpick, apply an even coat of E6000 to the back side of the cabochon and glue the stone to the leather or textile surface. Allow the adhesive to dry for at least ten minutes.

2. Thread a single thread of Nymo or FireLine (approximately 5' to 6' [1.5 to 1.8 m] long) on a size 12 English beading needle. Wax the strand well. Tie a knot at the end and cut, leaving about a ¼" (6 mm) tail.

3. Pass the needle up through the fabric from the underside, coming up next to the stone. String on six cylinder beads and stitch back down through the fabric. Come back up between beads 3 and 4, and then pass through beads 4, 5, and 6 again to create a backstitch **(a)**.

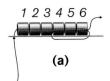

(a)

4. Continue backstitching around the perimeter of the stone, making sure that you finish with an even number of beads. Travel through the entire perimeter of the beads one more time to ensure good tension.

5. Begin peyote-stitching upward from the base row (see page 18). Coming out of a cylinder bead, pick up another cylinder bead, skip the next bead in the base row, and then go through the bead after that. Repeat this process of "pick up a bead, skip a bead, go through a bead" all the way around the base row. When you reach the end of this first row of peyote stitch, remember you will need to step up before beginning the next row **(b)**.

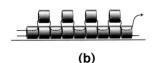

(b)

Continue peyote-stitching with cylinder beads for a couple of rows, until you reach the curve in the cabochon. At this point, switch to 15°s. This decrease in bead size will cause the bezel to curve inward, creating a tight fit to the stone **(c)**.

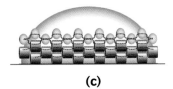

(c)

6. After you have bezeled up as high on the stone as you'd like, weave the thread back through to the base row and go through to the back side of the leather. Knot off on the back side with a couple of half hitches. Cut the thread, leaving about a ¼" (6 mm) tail.

7. If you wish, stitch a second "base row" around the bottom edge of the bezel with cylinder beads or 15°s to create an embroidery backstitch (six beads at a time). Pass through the entire row one more time, and stitch back through the leather, knotting off with a couple half hitches on the back side. This second row of embroidery around the base of the bezel is not necessary, but it adds a nice finished look to the bezeled stone and will also create a base row for adding embellishments around the stone **(d)**.

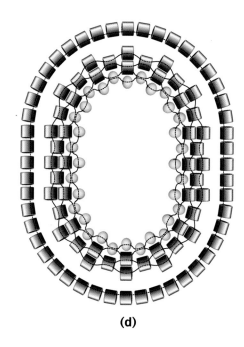

(d)

Technique 2: Open-Back Bezeling

This method works best for stones with pointed backs or any other type of irregular, non-flat back. Open-back bezels are created separately and then may be attached to a textile surface later or used without any textile backing. Like the first bezeling technique, this technique also uses peyote stitch and different bead sizes to tighten the bezel over the stone.

1. String a wingspan (a length as long as your open arms, approximately 5 feet [1.5 m]) of single-threaded FireLine on a size 12 English beading needle. Wax well.

2. Pick up enough cylinder beads to encircle the widest point of your stone. The circle of cylinder beads should be a perfect fit—not too loose, not too tight. You also want the count to be an even number. If it works out that a perfect fit is an odd number, then always add one additional bead, rather than subtract one. (The charts on pages 29–31 provides the counts for some of the basic rivoli crystal stones and other crystal stone shapes.) Tie the thread together with a square knot to form a circle of beads. Leave about 15" (38.1 cm) of thread as a tail.

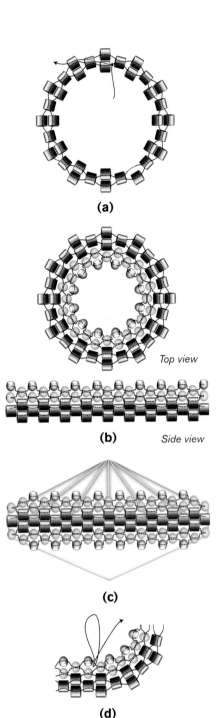

(a)

Top view

(b)   *Side view*

(c)

(d)

3. Go through two or three cylinder beads to hide the knot, and then begin peyote-stitching with cylinder beads. Travel all the way around to form a ring of peyote stitch that is three beads wide. At the end of the row, you will need to step up to begin your next row. Step up by passing through the first bead added in this row **(a)**.

4. Switch to 15°s. Peyote-stitch one to four rows with these beads (depending on the size of your stone). Pull in on your thread as you add each bead to create a cupped effect. You may keep the same color throughout or switch to a new color with each new row of beads. The number of rows of 15°s will depend not only on your stone size, but also on your tension.

   The chart is only a guide. It is always best to check the fit by popping the stone in place. This way, you will know whether or not you need another row of 15°s **(b)**.

5. Weave the final row with 15° Czech charlottes. When this row is complete, weave your thread up to the top-most row of cylinder beads, where you began the bezel. Pop the stone into the bezel, right side up, and hold it in place. Weave one to four rows of 15°s (again depending on the stone size and thread tension), finishing off with 15° Czech charlottes for the last row **(c)**.

6. When you have completed the bezel, half-hitch once or twice between the beads in the top row to hold everything tight. Leave the tails on the bezeled stone—you can work with these tails later on to attach stones or add embellishment to your beaded bezel **(d)**.

Tip: Correcting Tension

If you tend to peyote-stitch with tight tension, leave about one bead's width of thread in the initial circle of beads. This space will create a little slack to offset the tension.

Guidelines for Bezeling Rivolis

Rivoli size	Cylinder beads in initial circle	Back side	Front side
10mm	26 +1 row peyote	1 row 15°s 1 row charlottes	1 row 15°s 1 row charlottes
12mm	30 +1 row peyote	1 row 15°s 1 row charlottes	1 row 15°s 1–2 rows charlottes
14mm	36 +1 row peyote	2 rows 15°s 1 row charlottes	2 rows 15°s 1 row charlottes
16mm	40 to 42 +1 row peyote	2 rows 15°s 1 row charlottes	3 rows 15°s 1 row charlottes
18mm	46 +1 row peyote	2 rows 15°s 1 row charlottes	3 rows 15°s 1 row charlottes

Guidelines for Other Crystals*

Article # and shape	Cylinder beads in initial circle	Back side	Front side
4650 SQUARE RIVOLI, 14mm	42	2 rows 15°s 1 row charlottes	2 rows 15°s 1 row charlottes
4650 SQUARE RIVOLI, 18mm	52	2 rows 15°s 1 row charlottes	2 to 3 rows 15°s 1 row charlottes
4655 OCTAGON 16mm	44	2 rows 15°s 1 row charlottes	2 rows 15°s 1 row charlottes
LARGE OVAL 20 x 30mm	66	2 rows 15°s 1 row charlottes	3 rows 15°s 1 row charlottes
SMALL OVAL 13 x 18mm	40	2 rows of 15°s 1 row charlottes	1 to 2 rows 15°s 1 row charlottes
4439 SQUARE FRAME, 14mm	44	2 rows of 15°s 1 row charlottes	2 rows of 15°s 1 row charlottes

*NOTE: These numbers are intended as a general guideline. The count may vary slightly depending on bead size and tension.

Article # and shape	Cylinder beads in initial circle	Back side	Front side
1200 DENTELLE 60ss	36	2 rows 15°s 1 row charlottes	2 to 3 rows 15°s 1 row charlottes
1200 DENTELLE 65ss	40	2 rows 15°s 1 row charlottes	2 to 3 rows 15°s 1 row charlottes
1201 ROUND STONE, 17mm	40 to 42	2 rows of 15°s 1 row charlottes	2 rows 15°s 1 row charlottes
1201 ROUND STONE, 27mm	68	2 to 3 rows of 15°s 1 row charlottes	3 to 4 rows of 15°s 1 row charlottes
TRIANGLE 17mm	42	2 rows of 15°s (decreasing every 7th bead on 1st row) 1 row charlottes	2 rows of 15°s (decreasing every 7th bead on 1st row) 1 row charlottes
TRIANGLE 23mm	60	2 rows of 15°s (decreasing every 10th bead on 1st row) 1 row charlottes	2 rows of 15°s (decreasing every 10th bead on 1st row) 1 row charlottes

Chapter Six
Creating Closure

Taking the time to make a unique and beautiful beaded clasp, or closure, will greatly enhance your finished piece of jewelry. After all, details do make a difference. The projects in this book include four different types of beaded closures: a button with basic loop closure, a button with tab and beaded loop closure, a round beaded toggle closure, and a square beaded toggle closure.

Button with Basic Loop Closure for a Spiral Rope

An antique or new button makes a beautiful and unusual closure on a spiral rope, while at the same time finishing the spiral with a neat, tapered end. These directions are for finishing a basic spiral (with 11's as both the core and outer beads).

1. With the tail thread at the end of your completed spiral rope, pick up one "end bead" (a 4 mm or 6mm crystal bead works great). String five to seven 11° seed beads (a quantity equal in length to the radius of the button), one 4mm bead, and three 15°s. Slide the button on so that the shank slides up and over the 15°s. String another 4mm bead (to keep the button from sliding around) and five to seven more 11°s. Now come back up through the end bead and through three of the core beads in the spiral rope **(a)**.

2. Pick up three outer beads, then go back down through the end bead and through the 11°s, 4mm bead, 15°s (with button on them), 4mm bead, and 11°s to help reinforce the clasp attachment.

   Now go back up through the end bead again, this time through two of the core beads in the spiral rope **(b)**.

3. Pick up two outer beads, then go back down through the end bead and the 11°s, 4mm bead, 15°s (with button on them), 4mm bead, and 11°s again. Go back up through the end bead again, this time going through one of the core beads in the spiral rope **(c)**.

4. Pick up one outer bead, then go back down through the end bead and the 11°s, 4mm bead, 15°s (with button on them), 4mm bead, and 11°s **(d)**. After this final reinforcement, go back through the end bead one last time and weave off the tail by half-hitching several times in the outer beads.

   For the loop end of the clasp, after adding the end bead, string enough 11°s to create a loop that fits easily over the button at the other end of the necklace. Taper the spiral as described above.

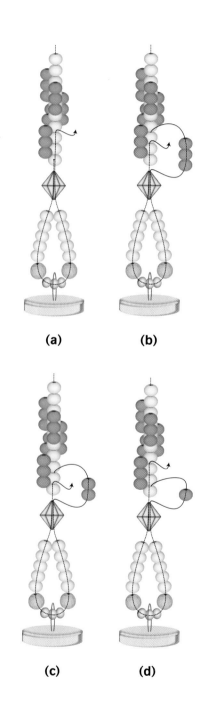

(a)   **(b)**

(c)   **(d)**

Button with Tab and Beaded Loop Closure

A button tab and a beaded loop make a beautiful and secure closure for all types of beaded bracelets.

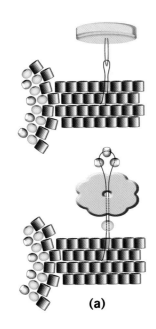

(a)

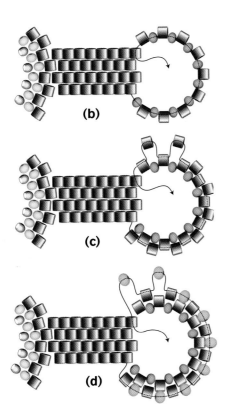

(b)

(c)

(d)

BUTTON TAB

1. Beginning with the button end, weave a tab of peyote stitch off of the last bezeled stone in the bracelet. This tab can be any width and length. (I usually make it about four beads wide by a length that is slightly longer than the button is wide.) Weave back to the middle of the tab and attach the button. Simply sew shank buttons in place.

2. If you're using a margarita or other button-type bead, pick up one 11° underneath the bead, then make a picot (see page 39) on top to hold it in place. The 11° creates a shank that will make it much easier for you to fasten the button **(a)**. Reinforce this attachment.

   You can embellish the edges of the button tab with picots of 15° seed beads or 15° charlottes. This finishing adds a nice detail and also covers up the thread along the edge of the peyote tab.

BUTTON LOOP

1. To create the loop, build a short tab that is equal in width to the button tab at the opposite end of the bracelet. Come out of the last row on one side of the tab, pick up a series of seed beads, alternating between 15° seed and cylinder beads. When you have strung up enough beads for a comfortable fit around the button (with a couple of extra beads), go back into the tab on the other side, creating a loop of beads **(b)**.

2. Now weave through the tab to the other side, where you began stringing, and begin peyote-stitching, adding a cylinder bead over every 15° **(c)**.

3. After you have completed this row, go back through the tab again, and step up to the outermost row of peyote stitch in this button loop. Make another row of peyote, this time with 11°s **(d)**.

4. Again, when you have completed this row of 11°s, weave back through the tab and step up again so you are coming out of one of these 11°s from the previous row. This time, make three-charlotte picots between every 11° to create a slightly ruffled edge **(e)**.

If the loop is a little too large for your button, weave back to the inside of the loop and do another row or two of charlottes around the inside for a better fit.

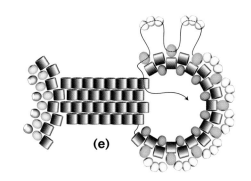

(e)

Round Beaded Toggle Closure

This toggle clasp is made entirely of peyote-stitched beads. There is no internal support. To create the toggle, begin with the toggle loop.

TOGGLE LOOP

1. String fifty cylinder beads on 5' to 6' (1.5 to 1.8 m) of thread. Leaving about a 15" (38.1 cm) tail, tie a square knot to form a loop of beads. Leave a length of thread one to two beads wide showing in the loop (two to three if you work with tight tension). Begin peyote-stitching. Do one row of cylinder beads, two rows of 15°s, and two rows of 15° charlottes, pulling in with each row to create a "cupping" effect.

2. When you've finished the first side, weave the working thread back to the top row of cylinder beads. Do two rows of 15°s and one row of charlottes, again pulling in with each consecutive row **(a)**. When the two sides are complete, the ring will look like an unmounted tire.

3. Finally, zip the last row of charlottes on this side to the last row of charlottes on the first side by zigzagging through the high beads of each row **(b)**. The zigzagging will pull the two sides together to form a solid loop.

4. Weave a tab off the middle row of cylinder beads. It should be two beads wide and twenty rows long (count ten beads up each side). Zip the last row of the tab to the middle row of cylinder beads on the loop, as shown in the drawing on the next page **(c)**. Embellish the edges of this tab loop with charlotte picots by coming out of one edge bead, adding three charlottes, and going through the next edge bead.

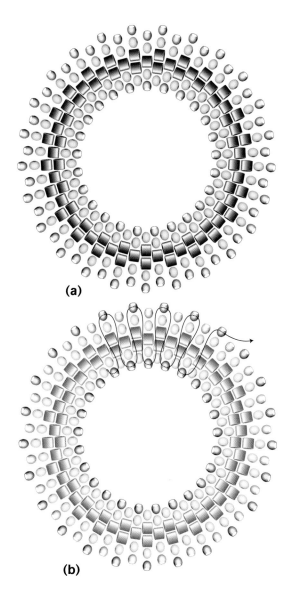

(a)

(b)

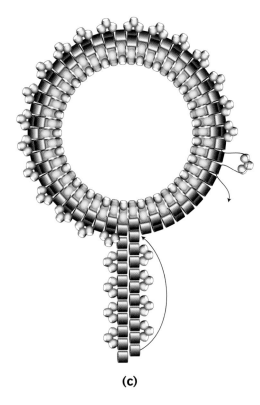

(c)

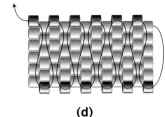

(d)

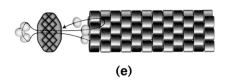

(e)

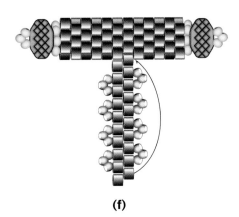

(f)

You may also embellish between every bead in the middle row of cylinder beads around the entire ring, creating a picot edging to the toggle ring. When the ring is complete, weave in both threads, half-hitching several times before cutting the tail **(c)**.

TOGGLE BAR

1. String twelve cylinder beads. Peyote-stitch back and forth. Weave a section that is twelve beads wide by twelve rows long (count six beads up either side). Zip the first row to the last row to create a tube **(d)**.

2. Coming out of one bead at one end of the tube, pick up one 15°, one 3mm to 6mm rondelle, and three 15°s. Go back through the rondelle to form a picot. Now pick up another 15° and go down through the next cylinder bead around the end of the peyote tube.

3. Do a U-turn within the tube and come back up out of the third bead around the end of the tube **(e)**. Pick up one 15°, go up through the rondelle, and through all three 15°s in the picot formed previously. Go back down through the rondelle and pick up one more 15°. Now go down through the fourth bead around the end of the tube. Repeat. Placing a 15° above each end bead centers the rondelle over the end of the tube.

4. After you have completed one end, weave your working thread down to the other end and repeat the process.

5. Weave to the center of the tube (sixth and seventh columns). Coming out of the fifth column, pick up one cylinder bead and go through the next bead in that row (the seventh column). Pick up another cylinder bead, and come back through the cylinder bead you previously added. Weave back and forth in this manner, creating a strip of flat even-count peyote that is two beads wide by twenty rows long (count ten beads up each side). Zip the last row of the strip to the base row on the tube. Embellish the edges with charlotte picots. Weave in threads, half-hitching several times before cutting the tails **(f)**.

Square Beaded Toggle Closure

With a couple of minor variations, the technique for the round toggle closure can be adapted to make a square toggle closure, which works nicely with square crystal stones. First, you must choose a number for the initial circle of cylinder beads that is divisible by four, resulting in an even number. Forty-eight would work, for example, because forty-eight divided by four equals twelve.

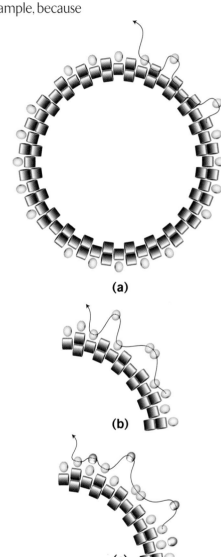

1. Begin as you would when making the round toggle (see page 35). Do the initial circle of cylinder beads and one round of peyote with cylinder beads. Now here's the tricky part: Begin peyote-stitching with 15°s—but you need to do four, evenly spaced decreases. In the case of a toggle that is forty-eight beads around, for example, this means you will need to leave out a bead in every sixth space. Go through the bead below this space to hide the thread and then step up again to the working row **(a)**.

(a)

2. When you have completed the first round of 15°s, do a second round of 15°s, this time putting two 15°s in the place of the gaps left in the previous row **(b)**.

(b)

3. When this row is complete, step up and do two rows of charlottes. On the first of these two rows of charlottes, pass through the two 15°s (used to create the decrease in the previous row) as if they were one bead **(c)**. Make the second row of charlottes as usual.

(c)

4. When you have completed the first side of the toggle, weave the thread up to the top row of cylinder beads and repeat the same pattern on the other side. Be sure to line up the decreases with the decreases on the other side. Add only one row of charlottes and zip this row to the second row of charlottes on the first side.

   As for the round toggle, make a connector loop to attach the toggle loop to the beadwork. The toggle bar for the square toggle is made the same as it would be for the round toggle (see page 36).

Chapter Seven
Embellishments

Embellishments add interest and dimension to any piece of woven beadwork. The decorative possibilities are endless, but the projects in this book rely on a few basic techniques. The instructions for each project indicate the embellishments for that project, but this chapter will give you an overview.

Picot Embellishments

"Picot" is a French term that means "little tip" or "little point." In beading, it is a type of embellishment formed by three seed beads. When you pass up and back through a previous bead or beads, you form a triangular shape, or point, with these three beads. It is one of the simplest forms of embellishment and is excellent for adding dimension and fine finishing to any piece of beadwork.

SIMPLE PICOT

There are several ways to make picots, depending on where and how your thread is coming out of the woven beaded base. You can make a simple picot when the thread is exiting from any place within the woven work. Pick up one bead (of any size) and then three seed beads (for the projects, always use three 15°s). Then do a U-turn and go back through the one bead in the opposite direction and back into the woven work **(a)**.

(a)

SIMPLE PEYOTE PICOT

The second type of picot is formed out of a peyote-stitch base. Make this picot when embellishing dimensionally off of a peyote-stitch surface. In several projects in this book, this picot adds a lacy, refined edging to bezeled crystal stones.

With a thread coming out of one "up" bead within the woven peyote, pick up three seed beads (for the projects, always use three 15°s), and go back into the next bead within the same row of peyote **(b)**.

(b)

TWO-BEAD BASE PEYOTE PICOT

When doing flat peyote stitch, whether even or odd count, you will find that the thread shows along the outer edge on either side of your work. The two-bead base peyote picot will cover this visible thread and finish the edge.

With a thread coming out of a bead along the outer edge of your woven peyote stitch, pick up three 15°s, and then go back down into the bead next to the one you exited **(c)**. You will have formed a picot shape. To make the next picot, come out of the next bead along the edge. Repeat until you have embellished the entire length of the outer edge of the flat peyote piece.

(c)

(d)

SINGLE-BEAD EMBELLISHMENT

The single-bead embellishment is a simplified version of the simple peyote picot. It is worked out of a peyote-stitch base and will add interest and dimension, but a less lacy effect than the simple peyote picot **(d)**.

CRYSTAL BURST EMBELLISHMENTS

Crystal burst embellishments will add a whole new level of sparkle and three-dimensionality to your woven work. They are relatively easy to make, but create much of the "bling" effect in many of the projects in this book.

(e)

These embellishments require 11° seed beads, a single crystal bead (bicone, round, etc.), and three 15°s. Coming out of the beadwork (whether a peyote-stitch bezel or the core of a spiral rope), pick up one 11°, one crystal bead, and three 15°s **(e)**. Go back through the crystal bead and the 11° and into the next bead in the woven base out of which you are working.

Tip: Making Crystal Bursts

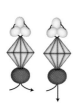

1. It's essential to keep tension on your thread. Otherwise the bursts will flop, rather than stand away from the work.

2. The 11° seed bead at the base of the crystal protects the thread from the sharp edges of the hole in the crystal bead.

3. Pull threads directly down out of the crystal bead—not on a diagonal—when cinching the embellishment to the base, or you could cut the thread on the sharp facets of the bead.

BRANCH FRINGE EMBELLISHMENTS

Branch fringe resembles tree branches or branches of coral. It is a simple technique that adds lushness and dimension to woven work. You can work branch fringe off of many woven stitches, including peyote stitch, spiral rope, and Ndebele. Here are two versions: crystal bead branch fringe and crystal drop branch fringe.

Crystal Bead Branch Fringe

This rich, coral-like fringe requires 11°s, 15°s, and round or bicone crystal beads. String a series of 11° beads (nine beads are shown here). Then pick up one crystal bead and three 15°s. Go back through the crystal bead and up through three of the 11°s.

Now pick up three new 11°s, a crystal bead, and three 15°s. Go back through the crystal bead and the three 11°s until you get back to the core of the beaded branch.

Go back up through three more of the core beads. Pick up three new 11°s, a crystal bead, and three 15°s. Go back through the crystal bead, the 11°s, and back into the core beads. Travel through the remaining three core beads back to the base of your work and weave back into it to secure your branch fringe **(f)**.

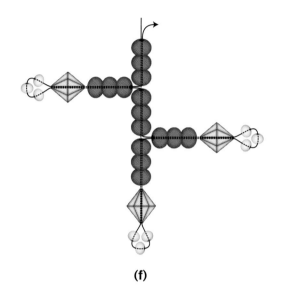

(f)

Crystal Drop Branch Fringe

This fringe is similar to the crystal bead branch fringe, but you work with crystal drop beads rather than round or bicone beads. It can be applied to all types of beadwork. This style of fringe is shown in the Crystal Dahlia Necklace on page 114.

Begin by stringing a series of 11° seed beads (five beads are shown here). Now string three 15°s, a crystal drop bead, and three more 15°s. Go back up through the last 11° and repeat the process by stringing three 15°s, a crystal drop bead, and three more 15°s. Then go up through the next 11°, and so on. This technique produces an even fuller fringe than the crystal bead branch fringe, forming a very organic, berrylike cluster **(g)**.

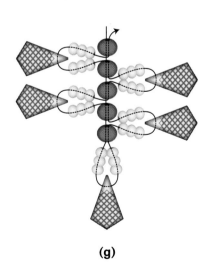

(g)

The Projects

CRYSTAL SPIRAL ROPE NECKLACE

Beading time varies, but count on at least 2 to 3 hours

The pink necklace is formed with a variation of a basic spiral rope, incorporating crystal bicones with Japanese 11° and 15° seed beads. You can work with either 3mm or 4mm bicones. Another great choice would be 3mm or 4mm faceted round crystals (#5000).

Step 1: Creating the Spiral Rope

Begin by threading as much FireLine as you can work with comfortably. A spiral works the same from either direction, so if you start with a long length of thread (two to three wingspans), you can wrap about one-half of the length onto a no-tangle bobbin (see page 13).

The spiral begins with a basic start stitch. Each following stitch (spiral stitch) will be the same, creating a sparkling spiral that stacks up on itself the same way a spiral staircase wraps around a central pole.

To form the start stitch, pick up four 11° seed beads (the core beads), one 15° (color A), one 15° (color B), one crystal bicone (3mm or 4mm), one 15° (color B) and one 15° (color A). Now circle around and come back up through the first four 11°s, as shown in the drawing **(a)**. Hold this loop of beads in your hand so the core beads (the 11°s) are to the right and the 15°s and bicone (the outer beads) are to the left. Maintaining this orientation is key to creating a consistent and correct spiral.

MATERIALS

- 15° Japanese seed beads, 5 grams each of two colors (A and B)
- 11° Japanese seed beads, 5 grams of one color
- 3mm or 4mm crystal bicones (#5301) or faceted rounds (#5000), 2–3 gross
- six 4mm, 6mm, or 8mm crystal "end beads" (crystal bicones or rondelles [#5040])
- one button (crystal, metal, pearl/antique, or new) for closure

TOOLS AND NOTIONS

- size 12 English beading needles
- FireLine, 6 lb. test
- microcrystalline wax
- scissors

(a)

(b)

The spiral stitch is done by picking up one 11° (core bead) and the basic series of outer beads: one 15° (color A), one 15° (color B), one bicone, one 15° (color B), and one 15° (color A). Slide all the beads down to the spiral base. Count back four core beads, and come up through these core beads so that after you have made the thread pass, your working thread is coming out the top core bead. Flip this most recent spiral stitch over to the left and continue as described to create your spiral neck strap **(b)**.

Step 2: Adding the Closure

To attach a button closure, thread the tail from the end of your spiral rope. Pick up three 4mm, 6mm or 8mm crystal end beads, five to ten 15° seed beads, depending upon button size (the length of strung 15°s should equal the radius of the button), a 3mm or 4mm crystal bicone, three 11°s (with the shank of the button slid over them), another crystal bicone, and five to ten more 15°s. Go back up through the crystal end beads and through the last three core beads in the spiral **(a)**. If the button shank does not fit over the 11°s you can substitute three 15°s.

Now pick up one 15° (color A), one 15° (color B), one bicone, and one 15° (color B). Go back through the already existing end beads, the 15°s, crystal bicone, three 11°s (with the shank of the button slid over them), the second crystal bicone, and the remaining 15°s. Go back down through end beads and through the last two core beads in the spiral **(b)**.

Now pick up one 15° (color A), one 15° (color B), and one 11° (in place of the bicone, as the bicone is sharp and could cut the thread). Go back through the already existing end beads, 15° seed beads, crystal bicone, three 11°s (with the shank of the button slid over them), the second crystal bicone, and the remaining 15°s. Go back up through end beads and through the last core beads in the spiral **(c)**.

(a)

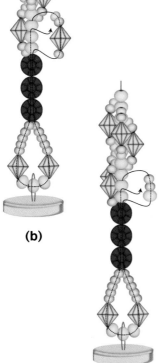

(b)

(c)

Now pick up one 15° (color A) and one 15° (color B). Go back through the already existing end beads, the 15°s, crystal bicone, three 11°s (with the shank of the button slid over them), the second bicone, and the remaining 15°s. Go back up through the end beads and weave the thread off in the spiral rope, half-hitching several times before cutting the tail.

Repeat the process on the other end of the rope, but rather than adding the beads and the button, add a series of 15°s, 11°s, and bicones long enough to fit comfortably around the button closure.

VARIATIONS

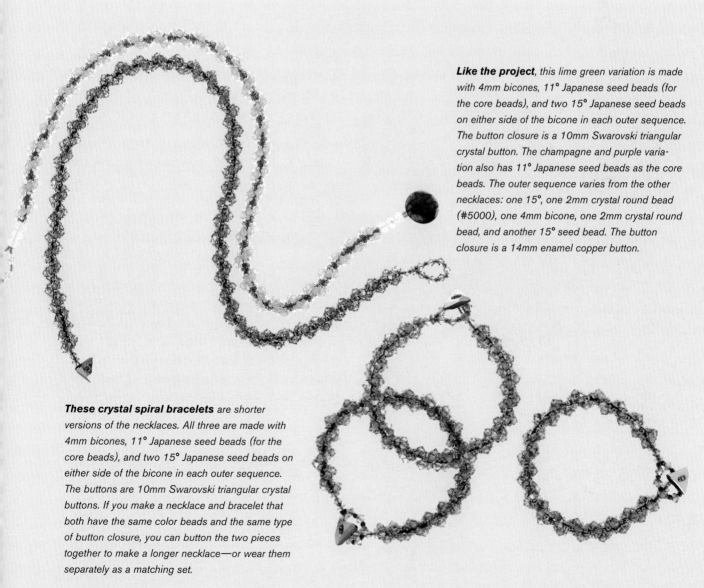

Like the project, this lime green variation is made with 4mm bicones, 11° Japanese seed beads (for the core beads), and two 15° Japanese seed beads on either side of the bicone in each outer sequence. The button closure is a 10mm Swarovski triangular crystal button. The champagne and purple variation also has 11° Japanese seed beads as the core beads. The outer sequence varies from the other necklaces: one 15°, one 2mm crystal round bead (#5000), one 4mm bicone, one 2mm crystal round bead, and another 15° seed bead. The button closure is a 14mm enamel copper button.

These crystal spiral bracelets are shorter versions of the necklaces. All three are made with 4mm bicones, 11° Japanese seed beads (for the core beads), and two 15° Japanese seed beads on either side of the bicone in each outer sequence. The buttons are 10mm Swarovski triangular crystal buttons. If you make a necklace and bracelet that both have the same color beads and the same type of button closure, you can button the two pieces together to make a longer necklace—or wear them separately as a matching set.

CRYSTAL CASCADE PENDANT

Beading time varies, but count on at least 3 to 5 hours

This pendant presents one of the many possible ways to incorporate bezeled crystal stones into bead jewelry. You can also vary the stone sizes for different effects. The pendant can be worn on a neck wire or on any other type of neck strap—including leather or silk cording, strung beads, or a beaded spiral rope. The instructions are for three graduating sizes of round stones, but you could also substitute one or more square crystals. The photograph shows a 14mm square stone (#4650) in the middle.

MATERIALS

- 27mm crystal stone (#1201)
- 18mm rivoli (#1122)
- 14mm rivoli (#1122)
- 11° Japanese cylinder beads, 5 grams of one color
- 15° Japanese seed beads, 2 grams of three different colors
- 15° Czech charlottes, 5 grams of one color
- metal neck wire, chain, or cording

TOOLS AND NOTIONS

- size 12 English beading needles
- FireLine, 6 lb. test
- microcrystalline wax
- scissors

Step 1: Bezeling the Crystal Rivolis

The first step is to bezel the crystal stones. Bezel the 14mm rivoli, 18mm rivoli, and 27mm round stone with technique 2 on page 27.

Step 2: Linking and Embellishing the Bezeled Stones

To connect the bezeled stones, weave one of the tail threads on the 18mm rivoli down to the middle row of the three rows of cylinder beads at the center of the bezel. Coming out of one of these bezel beads, pick up a cylinder bead and go through the next cylinder bead in the row. Repeat so that you now have two cylinder beads that "stand out" from the bezel.

Pick up a bead, and peyote-stitch back the other way, creating a tab that is four beads wide. Continue peyote-stitching back and forth until you have completed four rows of peyote stitch (count two beads up each side).

(a, step 2)

(a, step 3)

Now zip this tab into the 14mm bezeled rivoli by zigzagging through the high beads. After the tab is zipped, use this thread to edge the 14mm rivoli with picots made with three charlottes placed between every bead in the middle row of cylinder beads. Make picot embellishments on both sides of the connector tab linking the two stones together.

After you've completed the edging on the 14mm rivoli and on the connector tab between the stones, weave in the thread by half-hitching between beads and then cut off the tail close to the work.

Now create a tab on the other side of the 18mm rivoli—directly across from the first tab and also four beads wide by four rows. Zip the 18mm rivoli to the 27mm bezeled stone with this tab.

Use the tail threads to edge both the 18mm rivoli and the 27mm stone with 15° charlotte picots. You can go ahead and do the 18mm rivoli and connector tab, but you will have to make your bail (the tab that will loop over the necklace cord) on the top stone before you picot it, so leave the bail area free **(a)**.

Step 3: Creating the Bail

To create the bail, stitch up to the top of the 27mm stone. Starting slightly off of center top, in the middle row of cylinder beads, begin a small width of flat, even-count peyote stitch (six beads wide, three across and three back). Create a tab of peyote stitch approximately twenty-four rows long (count twelve beads up each side). When you have completed this tab, fold it back and zip the last row to the first row **(a)**.

After you've made the bail, finish picoting around the 27mm stone with 15° charlottes and embellish the edges of the bail with picots. After you've completed all the embellishment, weave off your tails, half-hitching several times before cutting the thread.

String your completed pendant on a neck wire, cord, or beaded neck strap.

This pendant is similar to the project pendant, but it was made with a 16mm Saturn rivoli, a 14mm light vitrail rivoli, and a 12mm crystal AB rivoli. The smaller overall stone sizes give this variation a more delicate feel.

These three floral-glass cabochon pendants are variations of the crystal cascade pendant. They are made the same way as the crystal pendants, except that you bezel the topmost cabochon on leather, working with the first bezeling technique (page 26). The other two stones are open-back bezeled, and then all three are linked together.

The finished pendants are strung on strips of leather with peyote-stitch beaded beads on both sides of the pendant. The strands are tied to close.

Tip: Varying Stone Size

Create a smaller, more delicate pendant by substituting 18mm, 16mm, and 14mm rivolis, or 18mm, 16mm and 12mm rivolis. You can also use a cabochon or button (with the shank removed) as the top stone in the pendant. In this case, bezel the top stones on leather (see page 26).

CRYSTAL CASCADE EARRINGS

Beading time varies, but count on at least 3 to 4 hours

These earrings are a simplified version of the Crystal Cascade Pendant (see page 48). You can wear them with the necklace or by themselves. For this style of earring, I recommend French wires. You could also attach posts to the back side of the top rivoli with a five-minute epoxy glue.

Step 1: Bezeling the Stones

The first step is to bezel the rivolis. Bezel two 12mm rivolis and two 16mm rivolis (one of each for each earring) with technique 2 on page 27. After you capture each stone, half-hitch once at the top of the stone to hold your threads tight.

MATERIALS

- two 16mm rivolis (#1122)
- two 12mm rivolis (#1122)
- 11° Japanese cylinder beads, 5 grams of one color
- 15° Japanese seed beads, 1 gram each of three colors
- 15° Czech charlottes, 3 grams of one color
- silver- or gold-filled French-hook ear wires

TOOLS AND NOTIONS

- size 12 English beading needles
- FireLine, 6 lb. test
- microcrystalline wax
- scissors

(a, step 2**)**

Step 2: Linking the Stones

To connect the bezeled stones, weave one of the tail threads on the 16mm rivoli down to the middle row of the three rows of cylinder beads at the center of the bezel. Coming out of one of these middle-row beads, pick up a cylinder bead and go through the next cylinder bead in the row. Pick up a bead and peyote-stitch back the other way so as to create a tab that is two beads wide by two rows long. Now, zip this tab into the 12mm bezeled rivoli by zigzagging through the high beads **(a)**.

Step 3: Embellishing the Edges

After the tab is zipped in place, use the thread to edge the 12mm rivoli with 15° charlotte picots, placing three charlottes between every bead in the middle row of cylinder beads.

When you've completed the edging on the 12mm rivoli and the connector tab between the stones, edge the 16mm rivoli just as you did the 12mm rivoli. When you reach the top center point of the 16mm stone, rather than doing a picot, pick up nine charlottes before going through the next cylinder bead. These charlottes will form a loop for attaching the French hook.

When you have embellished the entire edge of both stones and the connector tab, weave in the tails by half-hitching between beads and then cut off the thread close to the work.

Step 4: Attaching the Ear Wires

After you have linked and embellished both sets of stones, you are ready to attach the French hooks. With a small pair of chain-nose pliers, pry open the loop at the bottom of the French hook. Slide the loop of charlottes at the top of the bezeled stones over this open loop and then close the loop with the pliers **(a)**.

(a, step 4**)**

THAT'S A WRAP BRACELET

Beading time varies, but count on at least 12 to 15 hours

This bracelet is designed to teach you how to bezel small Austrian crystal stones with open-back bezels and then link them together to make a beautiful, wrap-around, tie-on bracelet. This was my first-ever kit of the month for my online bead club.

Step 1: Bezeling the Stones

The first step is to bezel the rivolis. Bezel twenty-seven 10mm rivolis (or 12mm rivolis, if you prefer) with technique 2 on page 27.

Step 2: Linking the Stones

After you have bezeled the rivolis, you are ready to link them together. Working with one of the tails left over from bezeling each stone, weave down to the center row of cylinder beads on the bezel.

MATERIALS

- twenty-seven 10mm Swarovski rivolis (#1122), 15 of one color, 12 of another color
- 11° Japanese cylinder beads, 6 grams each of two colors
- 15° Japanese seed beads, 6 grams each of two colors
- 15° Czech precious metal charlottes, 5 grams of one color
- 11° Japanese seed beads, 5 grams of one color
- two strips of goat thong (each 12" long by ¼" [30.5 cm by 6 mm] wide)

TOOLS AND NOTIONS

- 12 English beading needles
- FireLine, 6 lb. test
- microcrystalline wax
- scissors

57

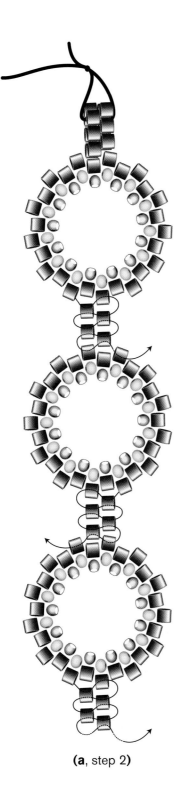

Pick up one cylinder bead and go through the next up cylinder bead in the center row. Pick up another cylinder bead, and pass back through the first one you added. This stitch will create a tab that is two beads wide **(a)**. Weave back and forth one more time to create a tab that is four rows long (count two beads up each side).

Now zip the tab into the next rivoli by zigzagging between the high beads in the tab and the high beads in the middle row of cylinder beads on the next rivoli. When you have zipped the first two bezeled stones together, secure the connection by half-hitching once between the beads.

Weave across to the other side of the second stone and create another tab to link it to the third stone. You will need to leave eleven beads and spaces across the middle row of cylinder beads between the tabs in order for the tabs to line up properly.

If your tab is starting one bead off from where it should be, weave through the cylinder beads and bypass the area where the tab would be. Then do a U-turn and come back from the other direction **(b)**. This process will shift the work by one bead, and your tab will now be properly aligned.

(b, step 2**)**

(a, step 2**)**

Step 3: Creating the Loops at the Ends

When you have linked all twenty-seven rivolis, you will create loops at each end of the chain to accommodate the thong closure. To create these loops, begin a tab as you did when connecting the rivolis—but make the tab longer (about twelve rows rather than just four).

When you've created the twelve-row tab (count six beads up each side), fold back the tab and zip it into its own first row to form a loop. Repeat at other end of chain.

Step 4: Embellishing the Edge

To add interest, embellish the piece with a simple edging created from charlottes and 11° seed beads. Single-thread about two wingspans of FireLine onto a needle. Begin by half-hitching the thread into the beadwork at one end of the bracelet. Then embellish as follows:

along tabs and at the end loops: Come out one cylinder bead, add three 15° charlottes, and then go back into the next cylinder bead **(a)**.

along rivolis: Pick up one 11° seed bead between every up bead in the center row of cylinder beads **(b)**.

(a, step 4)

(b, step 4)

Step 5: Attaching the Thong

The final step is to add the two goat-skin thongs to the ends of the piece. To add a thong, thread it through the loop at the end of the bracelet and tie with an overhand knot. Add the second thong at the other end **(a)**.

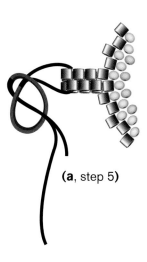

(a, step 5)

ART NOUVEAU NECKLACE

Beading time varies, but count on at least 14 to 16 hours

This necklace was created for a weeklong retreat at Hacienda Mosaico in Puerto Vallarta, Mexico. The design was inspired by the beautiful filigree jewelry of the early Art Nouveau period.

You will need at least two different sizes of crystal stones. I used vintage square faceted (8mm) stones in aquamarine and vintage baguette (rectangular) faceted (10mm x 16mm) stones in peridot. Work with any sizes and shapes you like. Circular, oval, even triangular crystal stones would be fine, too.

I used ten aqua stones and nine peridot stones, but your choice depends both on what size stones you have and on how long you want the necklace to be. Lay out your stones to get a better idea of the finished length. If you're not sure, get about one dozen of each type of stone—more is always better than not enough.

MATERIALS

- Crystal stones, number will vary
- 11° Japanese precious metal cylinder beads, 20 grams
- 15° Japanese seed beads, 10 grams
- 15° precious metal charlottes, 15 grams
- freshwater pearls (one for each larger stone and 20 to 30 as spacers [depending on finished length] between each stone)

TOOLS AND NOTIONS

- 12 and 13 English beading needles
- FireLine, 6 lb. test
- microcrystalline wax
- scissors

Step 1: Bezeling the Stones

The first step is to bezel all the stones. You can work with any size stone you like, ranging in size from 10mm to 18mm. You can also choose a variety of different stone shapes. Bezel the stones with technique 2 on page 27.

After you have bezeled the stones, weave in both the working thread and the tail thread, half-hitching several times before cutting the threads.

Step 2: Creating the Toggle Closure

The toggle clasp is composed entirely of different sizes of seed beads. To make the toggle, follow the instructions on page 35 in chapter six.

Step 3: Linking the Stones

When you have finished the clasp, you are ready to link the pieces. Double-thread a piece of FireLine. The stones are linked, edged, and embellished all in one fell swoop **(a)**.

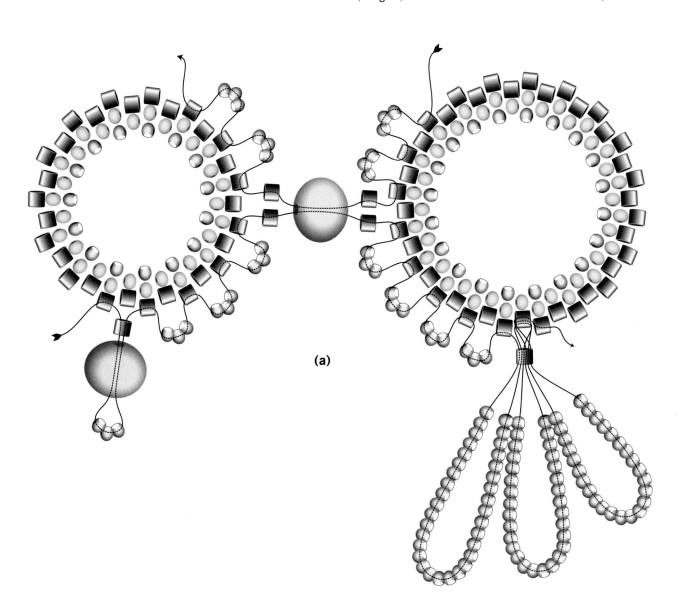

(a)

The cylindrical connector beads in the project necklace—on either side of the red pearls—are extremely rare, antique 24K gold French torse beads. Orange and green cylinder beads, found in this variation, are an excellent substitute.

This variation was made with 14mm Sahara rivolis, 10 x 12mm antique German tin-cut crystals in an orange fire-opal color, and one 14mm square #4652 stone (at center front). There are also different-colored seed beads. The connector pearls are 6–7mm mauve freshwater pearls. The embellishment pearls are 6mm burgundy freshwater pearls. In this variation, the cylindrical connector beads are Japanese cylinder beads.

CRYSTAL BURST EARRINGS

Beading time varies, but count on at least 3 to 4 hours

With this project, you'll learn how to create an open-backed bezel for cabochons and crystal stones that are without holes or that have irregular shapes. Work with Swarovski rivolis (#1122) in 14mm, 16mm or 18mm. You can also make these earrings with any number of other crystal stones, including square rivolis (#4650), oval stones, or even triangular stones. As with the Crystal Cascade Earrings, I recommend French wires for this style. You could also attach posts to the back side of the rivolis with a five-minute epoxy glue.

Step 1: Bezeling the Rivolis

The first step is to bezel the two stones. You can work with 14mm, 16mm, or 18mm rivolis (or another stone shape), depending on how large you want your earrings to be. Bezel the stones with technique 2 on page 27.

MATERIALS

- two Swarovski crystal rivolis, 14mm, 16mm or 18mm (#1122), or any variety of crystal stones in this range
- 11° Japanese cylinder beads, 5 grams of one color
- 15° Japanese seed beads, 1 gram each of three colors
- 15° Czech charlottes, 3 grams of one color
- 11° Japanese seed beads, 1 gram of one color
- 3mm/4mm crystal bicones (#5301), AB colors suggested, about 35 to 50 per earring (depending on stone size). AB refers to a shiny finish applied after the crystal is cut.
- two French-hook ear wires (sterling silver, surgical steel, or gold filled)

TOOLS AND NOTIONS

- size 12 English beading needles
- FireLine, 6 lb. test
- microcrystalline wax
- scissors

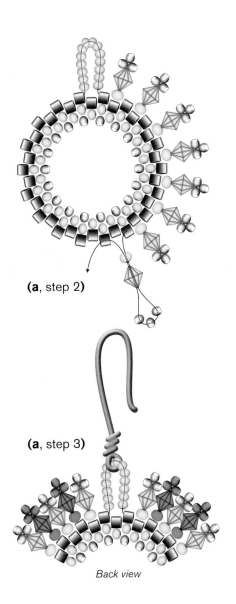

(a, step 2)

(a, step 3)

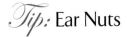

Back view

Step 2: Adding the Embellishments

Bring a thread out from the center row of cylinder beads. Add an embellishment between every cylinder bead in the center row. Pick up one 11°, one 4mm bicone, and three charlottes. Go back through the bicone and 11° (to create a picot of the charlottes) and go back into the next cylinder bead along the middle row **(a)**. At some point along this row, pick up fourteen 15°s (rather than repeat the established sequence) and go through the next cylinder bead. The 15°s will form a loop for attaching the French hook.

Finish the earring by adding a second row of embellishments to the inner row of cylinder beads on the front of the bezel. Use 3mm bicones in place of the 4mm bicones for this second row. Use crystals all the way around, placing one in front of the loop you made for the ear wire in the first row.

Step 3: Attaching the Ear Wires

With a small pair of chain-nose pliers, pry open the loop at the bottom of the French hook. Slide the loop of charlottes at the top of the bezeled stones over the loop and close the loop with the pliers **(a)**.

Tip: Ear Nuts

You may want to add "ear nuts" on the backs of the French hooks when you wear the earrings to keep the hooks from slipping out of your ears.

VARIATIONS

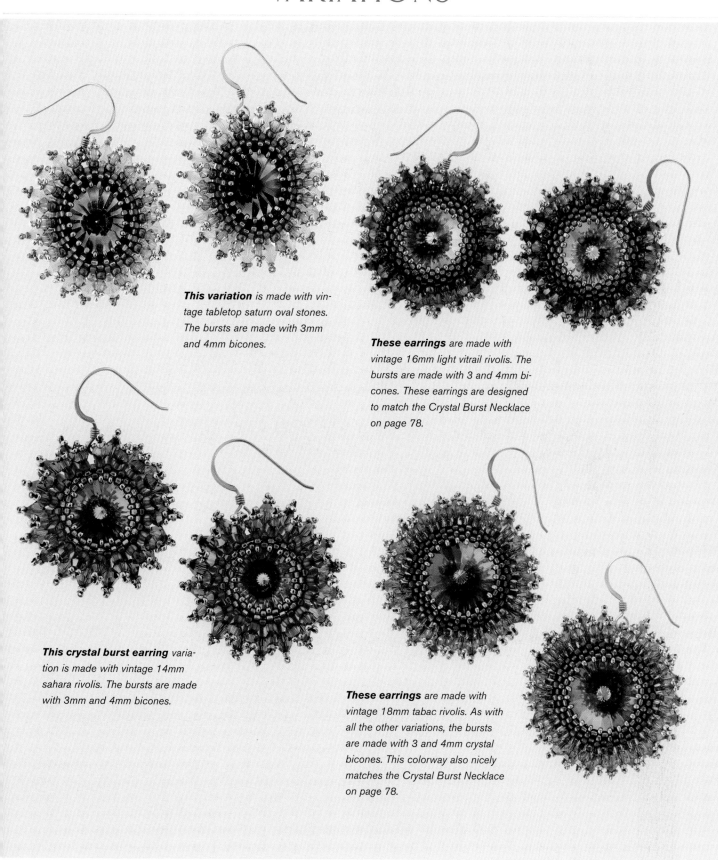

This variation is made with vintage tabletop saturn oval stones. The bursts are made with 3mm and 4mm bicones.

These earrings are made with vintage 16mm light vitrail rivolis. The bursts are made with 3 and 4mm bicones. These earrings are designed to match the Crystal Burst Necklace on page 78.

This crystal burst earring variation is made with vintage 14mm sahara rivolis. The bursts are made with 3mm and 4mm bicones.

These earrings are made with vintage 18mm tabac rivolis. As with all the other variations, the bursts are made with 3 and 4mm crystal bicones. This colorway also nicely matches the Crystal Burst Necklace on page 78.

CRYSTAL BURST RING

Beading time varies, but count on at least 2 to 3 hours

As you did for the Crystal Burst Earrings (page 64), you'll create an open-backed bezel for Swarovski rivolis. Originally made into costume jewelry, rivolis add sparkle and a vintage touch to any beaded piece.

Step 1: Bezeling the Rivoli

The first step is to bezel the rivoli. Bezel the stone with technique 2 on page 27.

Step 2: Creating the Comfort Band

Coming out of the bottommost row of the three rows of cylinder beads, pick up a cylinder bead and go through the next cylinder bead in the same row. Repeat so you have two cylinder beads that stand out from the bezel. Reverse direction, pick up a bead, and peyote-stitch back the other way to create a tab that is four beads wide.

MATERIALS

- one Swarovski rivoli (#1122), 14mm, 16mm, or 18mm
- 11° Japanese cylinder beads, 5 grams of one color
- 15° Japanese seed beads, 1 gram each of three colors
- 15° Czech charlottes, 3 grams of one color
- 11° Japanese seed beads, 1 gram of one color
- 3mm/4mm crystal bicones, AB colors suggested, about 40 of each size (AB refers to a shiny finish applied after the crystal is cut)

TOOLS AND NOTIONS

- size 12 English beading needles
- FireLine, 6 lb. test
- microcrystalline wax
- scissors

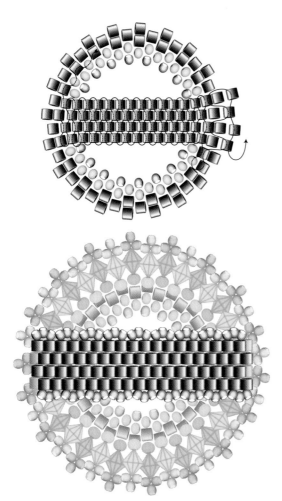

Continue working peyote stitch until the band reaches across the back of the bezel to the bottommost row of cylinder beads on the opposite side, directly across from where you began the tab. Weave back and forth between high beads in the band and the beads in the bottom row of cylinder beads on the bezel to zip the band into that row of cylinder beads **(a)**.

Step 3: Creating the Ring Band

Continue working peyote stitch four beads wide until you have created a band that will comfortably fit around your finger.

When the size is correct, attach the ring band to the point where you began weaving the comfort band off the bezel **(a)**. Working with charlottes, picot along the edges of the ring band and comfort band by adding three charlottes between each edge bead.

Step 4: Adding the Embellishments

Bring a thread out from the center row of cylinder beads. Add an embellishment between every cylinder bead in the center row. Pick up one 11°, one 4mm bicone, and three charlottes. Go back through the bicone and 11° (to create a picot of the charlottes) and go back into the next cylinder bead along the middle row **(a)**.

When you have completed this first row of embellishments, finish the ring by adding the second row in the inner row of cylinder beads. Use 3mm bicones instead of 4mm bicones.

(a, step 2**)**

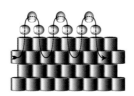

(a, step 3**)**

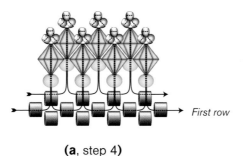

First row

(a, step 4**)**

VARIATIONS

The center stone is a vintage 16mm volcano rivoli, *with cylinder beads, three colors of 15°s, gold charlottes, and bicones.*

A vintage sphinx blue-green rivoli *serves as the center stone. This variation has a thinner ring band (two beads wide) and a row of 2mm crystal beads along the inside edge of the 3mm bicones.*

This variation has a vintage spring green sahara rivoli *at the center. It uses cylinder beads, bicones, two colors of 15°s, and copper charlottes.*

This 18mm vintage atlas rivoli *is gray-blue with a topaz center point. It is used with cylinder beads, three colors of 15°s, marcasite charlottes, and bicones. Note also the aqua nail head (vintage flat glass bead) sewn to the back side of the ring band.*

CRYSTAL BURST BRACELET

Beading time varies, but count on at least 15 to 20 hours

I designed this project to demonstrate how vintage crystal stones—which, until recently, have not been used much in woven beadwork—could be made into beautiful jewelry. The bracelet was a finalist in Swarovski's 2006 Create Your Style design competition and is now in the company's permanent collection.

Step 1: Bezeling the Rivolis

The first step is to bezel the rivolis. You can work with 14mm, 16mm, or 18mm rivolis, or any combination of these sizes. Bezel the stones with technique 2 on page 27.

MATERIALS

- seven Swarovski rivolis (#1122), 14mm, 16mm, or 18mm
- 11° Japanese cylinder beads, 10 grams of one color
- 15° Japanese seed beads, 10 grams total of two to four colors
- 15° Czech precious metal charlottes, 10 grams of one color
- 11° Japanese seed beads, 5 grams of one color
- 3mm and 4mm crystal bicones (AB finishes recommended), about 3 gross total
- one 10mm margarita, antique metal, glass or crystal button (for closure)

TOOLS AND NOTIONS

- size 12 English beading needles
- FireLine, 6 lb. test
- microcrystalline wax
- scissors

Step 2: Connecting the Stones

Weave your thread down to the middle row of the three rows of cylinder beads at the center of the bezel. Coming out of one of these beads, pick up a cylinder bead and go through the next cylinder bead in the row. Repeat so that you have two cylinder beads that "stand out" from the bezel.

Pick up a bead, and peyote-stitch back the other way to create a tab that is four beads wide. Continue peyote-stitching back and forth until you have completed five rows of peyote stitch. You may want to make these connector tabs longer or shorter, depending on the finished size of the bracelet.

Zip this connector tab into the second bezeled stone by zigzagging through the up beads of each. Weave across to the other side of the second stone and create another tab to link it to the third stone (a).

Step 3: Adding the Closure

After you have connected all the stones, you are ready to add the closure. A 10mm margarita bead makes an excellent button. Make a peyote-stitched tab on one end of the bracelet that is four beads wide and twenty to twenty-two rows long or long enough to accommodate your button.

Embellish the edge of this tab with charlotte picots by adding three charlottes between each edge bead. Coming out of this tab, stack up an 11° seed bead, a margarita, and a picot of three 15°s to form a button. Reinforce this connection several times—closures are always stress points (a).

(**a**, step 2)

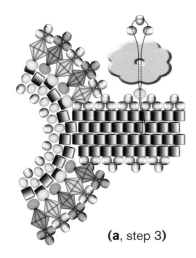

(**a**, step 3)

Now weave a single thread into the rivoli at the other end of the bracelet (the one without a tab). Create a loop to capture the button at the other end (see page 34).

Step 4: Adding the Embellishments

Now you are ready to add the crystal bicone embellishments. The first row of embellishments is one crystal burst between every cylinder bead of the central row of peyote stitch on each bezel.

Come out of one of these central cylinder beads, pick up one 11°, a bicone, and then three charlottes. Go back down through the bicone and 11° and through the next cylinder bead in the row. Repeat the process all the way around the bracelet, using 4mm or 3mm crystal bicones (or both!) **(a)**.

When you travel through the tabs that connect the bezels, embellish along their edges to create a fuller, more sparkly look. Add picot edging if you find that bicones in between the stones are crowding them.

The second row of crystal embellishments is the same as the first. Add it inside the initial row, between each cylinder bead in the topmost row of cylinder beads in each bezel.

(a, step 4**)**

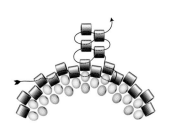

𝒯𝒾𝓅: Aligning the Tabs

If your tab is starting one bead off from where it should be, weave through the cylinder beads and bypass the area where the tab would be. Then do a U-turn and come back from the other direction. This process will shift the tab by one bead, and it will now be properly aligned.

VARIATIONS

This bracelet variation is made with vintage sphinx, sahara, medium vitrail, and tabac rivolis of various sizes, ranging from 14mm to 18mm. The bursts are made with 3mm rounds (#5000) on top and 4mm bicones (#5301) underneath. The button is a 12mm medium vitrail margarita.

This bracelet variation is made with 14mm olivine AB rivolis, 16mm aurum rivolis, and 17mm stones (#1201) in tourmaline and light smoke topaz. The bursts are made with 3mm and 4mm bicones. The button is a 10mm tabac margarita.

This bracelet is the first Crystal Burst Bracelet I ever made. The rivolis are 14mm and 18mm in volcano, cathedral, and atlas. The bursts are made with a variety of 3mm and 4mm bicones. In this piece, I used antique steel-cut beads rather than charlottes. The button is an antique steel-cut button that dates from the late 1800s.

This bracelet variation is made with 14mm and 18mm rivolis in volcano and sahara. The bicones in the bursts are all 4mm. The button closure is a 10mm volcano margarita.

This bracelet variation is made completely with sahara stones: two 14mm rivolis, an 18mm rivoli, a 27mm stone (#1201), one more 18mm rivoli, and two more 14mm rivolis. The bicones in the bursts are all 4mm.

CRYSTAL BURST NECKLACE

Beading time varies, but count on at least 30 to 40 hours

This stunning necklace is a variation on the Crystal Burst Bracelet (see page 72). As with the other crystal burst projects, you will make open-back bezels on each of the rivolis. You'll also learn how to angle the connections between the stones in order to give the necklace its proper shape and fit.

Step 1: Bezeling the Rivolis

The first step is to bezel the rivolis. You can use 14mm, 16mm, or 18mm rivolis, or any combination of these sizes. Bezel the stones with technique 2 on page 27.

Step 2: Connecting the Stones

Begin with the center rivoli in the necklace. Weave your thread down to the middle row of the three rows of cylinder beads at the center of the bezel. Coming out of one of these beads, pick up a cylinder bead and go through the next cylinder bead in the row. Repeat so that you now have two cylinder beads that "stand out" from the bezel.

MATERIALS

- eleven Swarovski rivolis (#1122), 14mm, 16mm, 18mm
- 11° Japanese cylinder beads, 5 grams each of four colors
- 15° Japanese seed beads, 24 grams total of four (or more) colors
- 15° Czech precious metal charlottes, 15 grams
- 11° Japanese seed beads, 10 grams total of one (or more) colors
- 3mm and 4mm crystal bicones (AB finishes recommended), about 5 gross total for front piece of necklace and an additional 1–2 gross for the back neck strap
- four 8mm round crystal beads
- two 6mm rondelles for toggle closure
- 2mm round crystal beads (#5000) for spiral rope, 2–3 gross

TOOLS AND NOTIONS

- size 12 English beading needles
- FireLine, 6 lb. test
- microcrystalline wax
- scissors
- velvet necklace bust (optional)

(a, step 2**)**

Peyote-stitch two beads back the other way to create a tab that is four beads wide. Continue peyote-stitching back and forth until you have completed seven rows of peyote stitch. Zip this connector tab into the next bezeled stone by zigzagging through the up beads.

Weave across to the other side of the second stone and create another tab to link it to the third stone. Angle the connections slightly to create a curve in the front piece of the necklace. The two sides will mirror each other in the placement of the tabs **(a)**. It is helpful to begin at the center and work out in either direction. (It may help to work with a velvet necklace bust to determine the right curve for the necklace.)

Step 3: Embellishing the Connected Stones

After you have linked the eleven rivolis, you are ready to add the bicone embellishments. Add them in the same way as you would for the crystal burst bracelet (see page 75).

When you are doing the first row of crystal embellishments, be sure to replace one crystal embellishment at each end of the necklace front piece with a loop of 15°s. The loops will allow you to attach the spiral neck strap **(a)**.

Step 4: Creating the Closure

Make a beaded toggle, as described on pages 35–36.

(a, step 3**)**

Step 5: Making the Spiral Rope Neck Strap

The neck strap on the back piece of this necklace is an embellished variation of the crystal spiral rope. The spiral rope itself is made with 11°s for the core and an outer sequence of one 15°, one 2mm round crystal (#5000), one 4mm bicone, one 2mm round crystal, and one 15° **(a)**.

The length of the spiral rope depends on the finished length of your necklace. You need to make two sections of spiral, one for each side of the necklace. Attach them to the sides of the front piece with an 8mm round crystal end bead and a loop of beads. The beads will thread through the loop at the end of the necklace front piece **(b)**. As you make the loop, taper off the spiral rope as described on pages 46–47.

Step 6: Attaching the Clasp

The clasp is attached as described on pages 46–47. Attach and taper off the spiral, as described. Then knot the threads and cut off the tails.

Step 7: Embellishing the Spiral Rope

The final step is to embellish the spiral rope. Thread a new needle with double-threaded FireLine and tie in the new thread, half-hitching a couple of times between the outer beads in the spiral. Weave up to one end of the spiral, so the thread is coming out between the first and second core beads.

The spiral is embellished between every core bead with one 11°, a 3mm bicone, and three charlottes. Go back through the bicone and the 11° to form a picot of the charlottes. Go through the next core bead and repeat **(a)**.

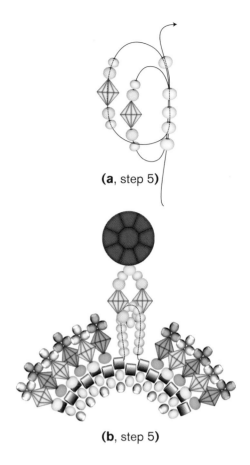

(a, step 5**)**

(b, step 5**)**

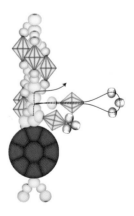

(a, step 7**)**

THREE-STRAND RIVOLI BRACELET

Beading time varies, but count on at least 12 to 15 hours

This bracelet is a slightly more formal version of the Bohemian-style That's a Wrap Bracelet shown on page 56. The precious-metal slide clasp and the alternately spaced rivolis add a touch of elegance and refinement to this bracelet.

Step 1: Bezeling the Rivolis

The first step is to bezel the rivolis. Work with twenty-nine 10mm rivolis (or 12mm rivolis, if you prefer). Bezel the stones with technique 2 on page 27.

Step 2: Linking the Stones

After you have bezeled the rivolis, you are ready to link them together. You'll make two chains of ten rivolis and one chain of nine rivolis.

MATERIALS

- twenty-nine 10mm Swarovski crystal rivolis (#1122)

- 11° Japanese cylinder beads, 5 grams each of three colors

- 15° Japanese seed beads, 12 grams of one color

- 15° Czech charlottes, 5 grams of one color

- 12° Japanese three-cuts, 5 grams of one color

- one 5-loop slide clasp (sterling silver or gold filled)

- two 6mm end beads (filigree with crystal [as shown] or another style)

TOOLS AND NOTIONS

- size 12 and 13 English Beading Needles

- FireLine, 6 lb. test

- microcrystalline wax

- scissors

(a, step 2**)**

Working with one of the tails left over from bezeling each stone, weave down to the center row of cylinder beads on the bezel. Pick up one cylinder bead and then skip over the ditch, going through the next "up" cylinder bead in the center row. Pick up another cylinder bead, and stitch through the first one you added in the ditch to create a tab that is two beads wide. Weave back and forth one more time to create a tab that is four rows long (two beads up either side).

Now zip the tab into the next rivoli by zigzagging between the "up" beads in the tab and the "up" beads in the middle row of cylinder beads on the next rivoli. Secure the connection by half-hitching once between the beads.

Weave across to the other side of the second stone and create another tab to link it to the third stone. You will need to leave eleven beads and spaces across the middle row of cylinder beads between tabs in order for them to line up properly **(a)**.

When you've created the first chain of rivolis, which is ten stones long, set it aside and make another. Make a third chain that is nine stones long. Do not make tabs on the ends of these chains—the chains will be attached to the clasp with a loop of beads.

Step 3: Embellishing the Edge

To add interest to this piece, embellish the three chains with a simple edging of charlottes and three-cuts. It's easier to make the embellishment before attaching the chains of rivolis to the clasp. Single-thread about one wingspan of FireLine onto a size 12 English beading needle. Begin by half-hitching the thread into the rivoli bezel at one end of the chain. Then embellish as follows:

along tabs: Coming out of one cylinder bead, add three size 15° charlottes and then go back into the next cylinder bead **(a)**.

along rivolis: Pick up one 12° three-cut between every "up" bead on the center row of cylinder beads **(b)**.

(a, step 3**)**

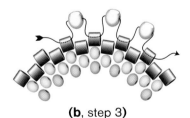

(b, step 3**)**

Step 4: Attaching the Clasp

After you have embellished the strands, you are ready to attach them to the clasp. The top and bottom chains (of ten rivolis each) are attached to the outermost loops on each side of the clasp with a simple loop of charlottes. Coming out of a cylinder bead of the center row of the bezel, string one 12° three-cut bead and about eleven charlottes and loop through the top soldered ring on the clasp. Go back through the 12° three-cut bead and then into the next cylinder bead in the center row on the rivoli. You may want to reinforce this loop a couple of times, because it is a stress point. Repeat the same process at the other end of this chain, then again at both ends of the second chain **(a)**.

The third chain, placed in the center of the two outer chains, is offset so that the rivolis in each chain alternate in position, rather than align. To create this effect, add a 6mm bead at each end of the chain. Make the attachment as you did for the outer chains, but pick up the 6mm bead on each end after picking up the 12° three-cut and before making the loop of charlottes.

After all the clasp attachments are completed and reinforced, weave off any tails, half-hitching a couple times before cutting the thread.

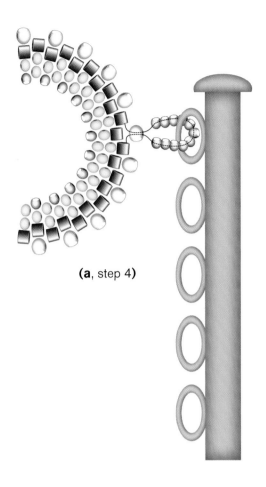

(a, step 4**)**

SQUARE-OFF BRACELET

Beading time varies, but count on at least 10 to 12 hours

This project was designed to teach you how to bezel square crystal stones with open-back, beaded bezels. It is made with vintage 14mm square crystal stone #4652, but there are many other options—for example, vintage square crystal stone #4650 or modern square crystal stone #4470.

Step 1: Bezeling the Stones

The first step is to bezel the seven 14mm crystal stones. Bezel each of these with technique 2 on page 27.

Step 2: Connecting the Bezeled Stones

Now you'll connect the bezeled stones with flat odd-count peyote. Working with one of the tails that is still attached to your stone, weave down into the middle row of cylinder beads. Coming out of a cylinder bead in this middle row, pick up one cylinder bead and then go through the next cylinder bead in the middle row. Repeat three more times so you have a total of four up beads that have been worked off the middle row of cylinder beads on one side of the bezel, as shown in **(a)** on page 88.

MATERIALS

- seven 14mm square Swarovski stones (vintage #4650 or 4652, modern #4470)
- 11° Japanese cylinder beads, 10 grams of one color
- 15° Japanese seed beads, 5 grams each of two colors
- 11° Japanese seed beads, 5 grams of one color
- 15° precious metal Czech charlottes, 5 grams

TOOLS AND NOTIONS

- size 12 English beading needles
- FireLine, 6 lb. test
- microcrystalline wax
- scissors

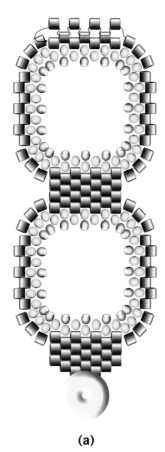

(a)

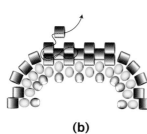

(b)

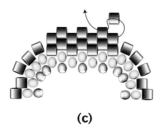

(c)

Because you are doing odd-count peyote, you need to do a U-turn within the bezel in order to come back through the fourth "up" bead **(a)**.

Pick up a cylinder bead and go through the third "up" bead. Then pick up another cylinder bead, and go through the second "up" bead. Finally, pick up a third cylinder bead and go through the first "up" bead. You have completed two rows of peyote stitch in the connector tab **(b)**.

To begin the third row of odd-count peyote, pick up a bead and then go through the "up" bead, as shown in the drawing. Work your way across, peyote-stitching as usual. When you get to the far side, you will again need to do a U-turn within the tab to come back around and through the far side so that you are ready to begin peyote-stitching again **(c)**.

Be sure you have created four rows (two times back and forth) of peyote stitch for your connector tab. Then line up the tab with the next bezeled stone and zip them together by zigzagging through the "up" beads on each piece. Afterward, tie off the tails to get them out of your way.

If you see that the tab is not centered when you try to zip it to the next stone, rotate the second stone 90° so it is. Repeat until you have connected all seven stones.

Step 3: Creating the Closure Mechanism

For the closure, you have a couple of options. Both styles are shown here.

The first option is to create a button closure like the one used on the Crystal Burst Bracelet (see page 74).

The second option is to create a square toggle closure (see page 37) with a thread coming out of the center 11° bead on the end of the bezel. Make a ring of nine 15° beads and secure. Repeat on the opposite end.

Now attach the clasp. With a thread coming out of the center of the toggle bar, string seven 11° beads and eleven 15° beads. Loop the strand through the ring attached to the bracelet, pass back through the seven 11° beads, and secure. Attach the ring end of the toggle clasp to the other end of the bracelet with a loop of nine 15° beads that pass through the loop on the bracelet.

Step 4: Embellishing the Bracelet

After the basic form of the bracelet is complete, an edge embellishment of gold charlottes and 11°s adds a nice detail without taking away from the beauty and the geometric shapes of the stones.

Thread about 5' (1.5 m) of single-threaded FireLine. Half-hitch a couple of times within the beadwork of the first stone to start the thread. Weave down to the middle row of cylinder beads (the same row you built the tabs from) and pick up one 11° bead before stitching through the next cylinder bead in the row **(a)**. This process will create a nice, studded look along the edge of each stone.

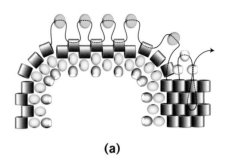

(a)

When you reach the tabs between the stones, you'll work a slightly different edging technique with the 15° gold charlottes. Coming out of the first cylinder bead along the edge of the tab, pick up three charlottes and go back down into the next cylinder bead along the edge of the tab. Turn around within the tab and pass back through the third charlotte in the picot. Pick up two more charlottes and go into the next cylinder bead along the edge of the tab. Repeat for the entire length of each tab.

VARIATION

This variation on the Square-Off Bracelet is made with seven 14mm (#4652) vintage stones in tabac. The stones are bezeled in delicas and 15° seed beads, and then embellished with custom-etched Japanese 11°s. The closure on this bracelet is a button-tab closure (see page 34). It is made with a 14mm enameled copper button.

Rings & Things Necklace

Beading time varies, but count on at least 12 hours

I designed this necklace for Beads on the Vine, a three-day bead retreat held in San Luis Obispo, California, in July 2006. This project provides a great way to incorporate beads, bezeled stones, beaded rings, and crystal spiral rope into a stunning necklace design. The finished piece is reminiscent of medieval adornment, reinvented with modern materials and color schemes.

The version shown at left uses 60ss dentelles in place of the 16mm rivolis, and 12mm rivolis in place of the 8mm stones. The rings are edged with single 11°s. The variation shown on page 95 uses the stones listed at right and the rings are edged with three-bead picots.

Step 1: Bezeling the Crystal Stones

The first step is to bezel the six crystal stones: three 16mm Swarovski crystal rivolis (#1122); two 8mm Swarovski crystal stones (#4650); and one 27mm Swarovski crystal stone (#1201). Bezel all stones with technique 2 on page 27.

MATERIALS

- three 16mm Swarovski crystal rivoli (#1122)
- two 8mm Swarovski crystal stones (#4650)
- one 27mm Swarovski crystal stone (#1201)
- three 13mm Swarovski crystal rings (#1245)
- 11° Japanese seed beads, 10 grams of one color
- 15° Japanese seed beads, 10 grams each of three colors
- Japanese cylinder beads, 10 grams of one color
- 15° Czech charlottes, 5 grams of one color
- six 6mm vintage Swarovski lentil beads (#335)
- ten 3mm cubic zirconia rondelles
- two gross 3mm or 4mm crystal bicones (#5301)

TOOLS AND NOTIONS

- size 12 and size 13 English beading needles
- FireLine, 6 lb. test
- microcrystalline wax
- scissors

Step 2: Creating the Beaded Rings

After bezeling the stones, you are ready to begin to peyote-stitch the beaded rings. There are three beaded rings in this design: two in the front and one in the toggle closure at the back. All three rings are made with forty-eight cylinder beads in the initial circle of beads. Make the rings, following the directions on page 35.

Finish the toggle ring with a connector loop and picots between every bead in the middle row of cylinder beads around the ring. At the same time, make the bar portion of the toggle closure, beginning with a strip of peyote stitch that is fourteen cylinder beads wide (see page 36).

For the other two rings (which will appear in the front portion of the necklace), embellish between every bead with three 15° charlottes in the middle row of cylinder beads around the entire ring, creating a picot edging.

Now create the center axis of beads in the rings. Come out of one of the charlottes along the inner center row. Pick up one 11°, one 3mm cubic zirconia rondelle, one 6mm crystal lentil, one 3mm cubic zirconia rondelle, and one more 11°. Go through the inner-row charlotte directly across from where the thread came out. Go back through all the axis beads and back into the original charlotte you exited **(a)**. When the axis is complete, weave in both threads, half-hitching several times before cutting the tail.

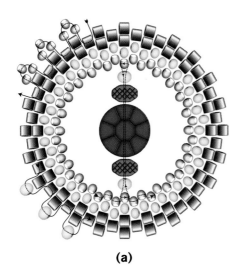

(a)

Tip: Change the Look

To create a bolder, simpler look on the embellished ring, use one 11° instead of three 15°s between every cylinder bead along the middle row, as shown in the drawing above.

Step 3: Linking Together the Stones and Rings

After you have completed the components of the neck-lace centerpiece, you are ready to link them together. All attachments are made with two-bead-wide tabs, made with even-count, flat peyote stitch out of the middle row of cylinder beads on each component. Either the tab is zipped to a second component, or the tab is looped around a ring and zipped back to the component out of which it was formed **(a)**.

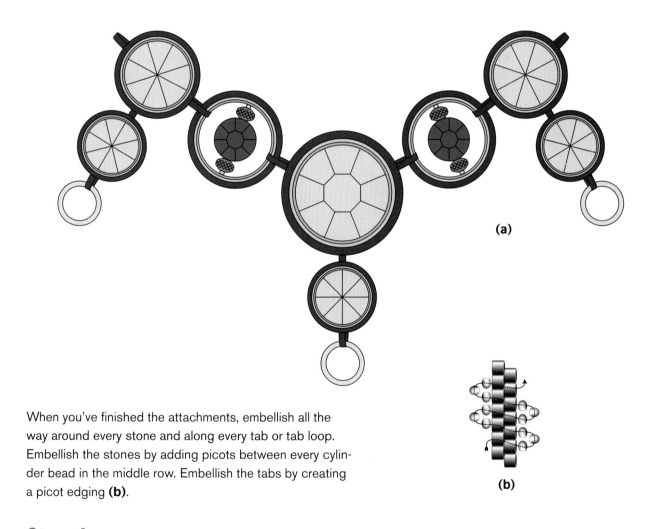

(a)

(b)

When you've finished the attachments, embellish all the way around every stone and along every tab or tab loop. Embellish the stones by adding picots between every cylinder bead in the middle row. Embellish the tabs by creating a picot edging **(b)**.

Step 4: Creating the Spiral Neck Strap

When you've finished assembling the stones and rings for the centerpiece, you are ready to weave the two spiral ropes that form the neck strap. This rope is made with a variation of the basic spiral rope (see page 45), with 11°s

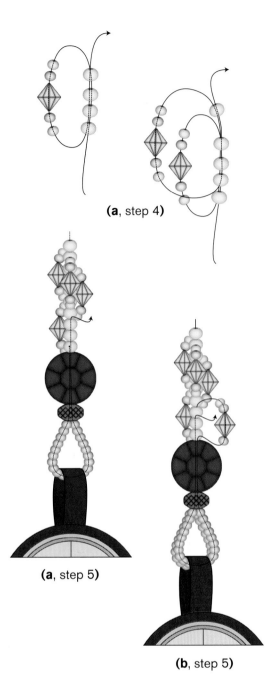

(a, step 4)

(a, step 5)

(b, step 5)

as the core beads. Follow this sequence for the outer beads: one 15° (color A), one 15° (color B), one 3mm or 4mm crystal bicone, one 15° (color B), and one 15° (color A) **(a)**.

The neck strap is actually two pieces of spiral rope, each connected to either side of the centerpiece of the necklace and attached to a toggle clasp at the back. (The necklace shown here required one gross of crystal for each side of the spiral rope.)

Step 5: Attaching the Spiral Neck Strap

After you've created the two spirals for the neck strap, you are ready to attach each section to the centerpiece of the necklace. Thread the tail end of your spiral rope. Pick up one 6mm crystal lentil bead, one 3mm cubic zirconia rondelle, and seventeen to twenty-one 15°s (depending upon bead size, as there is always some variation). Circle through the left connector loop on the centerpiece and go back through the 3mm rondelle, the 6mm crystal lentil, and the last three core beads in the spiral **(a)**.

Now pick up one 15° (color A), one 15° (color B), one bicone, and one 15° (color B). To reinforce the connection, go back through the crystal lentil and 3mm cubic zirconia rondelle, and through the loop of 15°s. Go back up through the 3mm cubic zirconia rondelle, through the lentil bead, and through the last two core beads in the spiral **(b)**.

Pick up one 15° (color A), one 15° (color B), one 11° (in place of the bicone, which is sharp and could cut the thread). Go back through the crystal lentil and 3mm cubic zirconia rondelle and pick up seventeen to twenty-one

15°s. Circle these beads through the connector loop on the centerpiece and go back through the 3mm cubic zirconia rondelle, through the 6mm lentil bead, and through the last core bead in the spiral **(c)**.

Now pick up one 15° (color A) and one 15° (color B). To reinforce the connection, go back through the 6mm lentil, the 3mm cubic zirconia rondelle, and around the second loop of 15°s you just made. Go back through the 3mm cubic zirconia rondelle, through the 6mm lentil bead, and weave the thread off in the spiral rope, half-hitching several times before cutting the tail **(d)**.

Repeat the process on the other side of the centerpiece, working with the second section of spiral rope.

Step 6: Attaching the Beaded Toggle Clasp

The clasp is attached to the spiral in the same way that the spiral is attached to the centerpiece of the necklace (see step 5). When you have attached both ends of the clasp, weave off the thread into the spiral, half-hitching several times before cutting the tail.

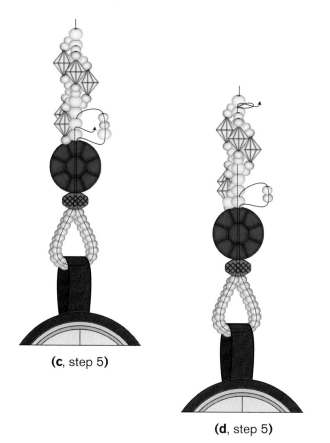

(c, step 5**)**

(d, step 5**)**

*This **Rings & Things** variation is another version of the project necklace. The outer row of the ring is embellished with a three-charlotte picot. It was made with a 27mm sahara (#1201), three 16mm sahara rivolis (#1122), two 8mm madeira topaz (#4650), and three sahara crystal rings (#1245). The bicones in the neckstrap are 4mm citrine cathedral. The toggle closure ring and the beaded rings at the front are embellished with 15° charlotte picots.*

INTERLOCKED NECKLACE

Beading time varies, but count on at least 10 to 12 hours

This necklace was designed with the new Swarovski frames (#4439) to interpret them in a unique and innovative way. The finished piece is reminiscent of Celtic knot work, reinvented with modern materials and color schemes.

Step 1: Bezeling the Stone

The first step is to bezel the center stone: either a 65ss dentelle or a 16mm rivoli. Bezel the stone with technique 2 on page 27.

Step 2: Adding the Primary-Color Frames

You will add the first four primary-color frames directly off of the center stone. Working with the thread you used to create the stone bezel, weave down to the center row of cylinder beads. Coming out of a bead in this center row, pick up a new cylinder bead and go through the next bead in that center row. This newly added bead will sit in the "ditch" between the beads in the center row.

MATERIALS

- seven 14mm Swarovski crystal frames (#4439) (4 primary color, 3 secondary color)
- one 65ss dentelle (#1200) or 16mm rivoli (#1122)
- 11° Japanese seed beads, 5 grams of one color
- 15° Japanese seed beads, 10 grams each of two colors
- 11° Japanese cylinder beads, 10 grams of one color
- 15° Czech charlottes, 4 grams of one color
- 3mm or 4mm crystal bicones (#5301), 2–3 gross
- four 8mm Swarovski rondelles (#5040)
- two 6mm Swarovski rondelles (#5040)

TOOLS AND NOTIONS

- size 12 English beading needles
- FireLine, 6 lb. test
- microcrystalline wax
- scissors

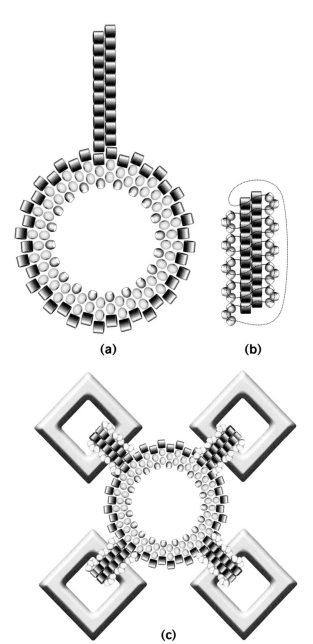

(a)

(b)

(c)

Now pick up another cylinder bead and go back through the first cylinder bead you added. Continue adding beads in this way, stitching back and forth, until you have created a strip of even-count peyote stitch that is two beads wide by twenty rows long (count ten beads up each side) **(a)**.

Circle this peyote strip around one of your primary-color frames. Be sure the frame is face up in relation to the center stone (it's easy to attach them upside down and not realize it until later, so double-check). When the frame is in place, zigzag through the "up" beads in each end to zip the end of the strip to the bezel beads out of which it began.

When you've attached the frame to the stone, embellish the connector loop. Zigzag back and forth across the peyote strip and picot both edges by coming out of one edge bead, picking up three charlottes, and going through the next edge bead on both sides of the strip **(b)**.

Now you are ready to attach the second frame. Weave over eight spaces and beads along the middle row of cylinder beads before starting your next tab. Be sure that there are eight spaces and beads (a space, a bead, a space, a bead, a space, a bead, a space, a bead) between each tab, to ensure proper spacing.

Repeat the process until you have attached all four frames and embellished their connector loops. Now weave off your threads, half-hitching several times within the beadwork before cutting off the tails **(c)**.

Tip: Adjusting Spacing

If your eighth space/bead is a space and not a bead, you are going in the wrong direction. Bypass where the tab would be and do a U-turn in the bezel so you are heading in the right direction. This process will shift the tab by one bead and correct the spacing.

Step 3: Adding the Secondary Frames

The central portion of the necklace is complete. Now you'll add the three secondary frames. Make six strips of even-count flat peyote that are each two beads wide by forty rows long (count twenty beads up each side).

Working with one of these strips, create an attachment loop around one of the secondary frames, zipping the end row of peyote stitch into the center of the tab (about the twentieth or twenty-first row in the tab) **(a)**. Half-hitch once or twice to keep the attachment tight and the thread from slipping.

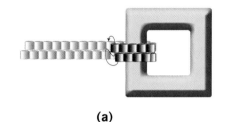

(a)

Now thread the tail thread on the other end of the tab. Loop the tab around one of the four primary frames attached to the central stone. Zip this end of the tab into the center of the tab, where you attached the first end (about the twentieth or twenty-first row) **(b)**. As you did with the primary connector loops, embellish the edges of this connector loop by picoting with charlottes.

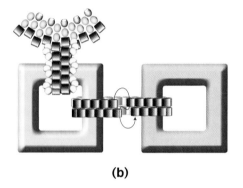

(b)

When you have completed the first connector tab on this secondary frame, work with a second peyote stitch strip to link this frame to a second primary frame. Continue connecting and embellishing with picots until all six strips connect the three secondary frames (two connections per one secondary frame) **(c)**.

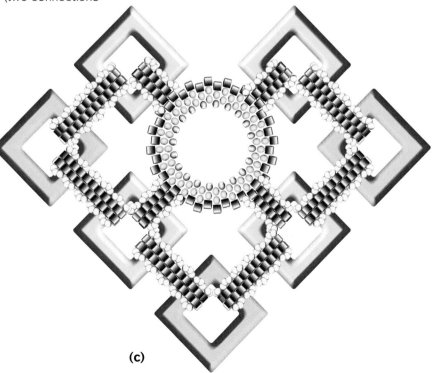

(c)

(a)

(b)

(c)

Step 4: Creating and Attaching the Neckstrap

When you have finished the crystal frame centerpiece, you are ready to weave the two spiral ropes that form the neck strap. This rope is the same as the basic spiral rope variation in the Crystal Spiral Rope Necklace.

Make two spiral ropes, one for each side of the necklace, following the directions on page 45. The length of these spirals will vary, depending on the finished length of the necklace. For a standard 18" (45.7 cm) necklace, you will need two 7½" (19 cm) sections of spiral rope.

When you have made the two spiral ropes, you are ready to attach them to the centerpiece of the necklace. Create the attachment by threading the tail end of your spiral rope. Pick up one 8mm crystal rondelle and seventeen to twenty-one 15°s (depending upon bead size, as there is always some variation). Circle through the left secondary frame on the centerpiece and go back through the 8mm rondelle and through the last three core beads in the spiral **(a)**.

Now pick up one 15° (color A), one 15° (color B), one bicone, and one 15° (color B). To reinforce the connection, go back through the crystal rondelle and through the loop of 15°s. Go back up through the 8mm rondelle and through the last two core beads in the spiral **(b)**.

Now pick up one 15° (color A), one 15° (color B), one 11° (in place of the bicone, which is sharp and could cut the thread). Go back through the crystal rondelle and pick up seventeen to twenty-one 15°s. Circle through the top left primary frame on the centerpiece and go back through the 8mm rondelle and through the last core bead in the spiral **(c)**.

Now pick up one 15° (color A) and one 15° (color B). To reinforce the connection, go back through the crystal rondelle and around the second loop of 15°s you just made **(d)**. Go back through the rondelle and weave off the thread in the spiral rope, half-hitching several times before cutting the tail. Repeat the process on the other side of the center-piece to attach the second spiral rope.

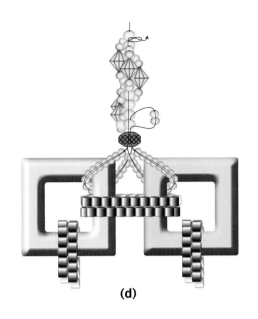

(d)

Step 5: Creating the Beaded Toggle Clasp

The toggle clasp at the back of this necklace is created entirely from peyote-stitched beads. There is no internal support. To make this toggle clasp, follow the instructions on page 35.

Step 6: Attaching the Clasp

You will attach the clasp to the spiral the same way you attached the spiral to the centerpiece of the necklace. The only difference is that, after you string the 8mm crystal, you put the loop of 15°s through the connector loop on the bar or loop of the toggle closure rather than through a frame.

Taper off the spiral as described in step 4, except put both loops of 15°s through the connector loop rather than into two separate frames. After you have attached both ends of the clasp, weave off the thread into the spiral, half-hitching several times before cutting the tail.

Tip: Lengthen the Strap

If you want a slightly longer spiral rope for the neck strap, simply add more crystal beads. Or you can replace the bicone in the outer beads at the back of the necklace with 11°s. Because the spiral is at the back side of the neck, the substitution won't show. You'll get the same spiral effect and a longer neck-lace, without buying additional crystals.

VARIATIONS

These three variations on the Interlocked Necklace were each made with only small changes in the materials, which produce a beautiful variety of effects.

This necklace variation was made with a vintage light siam AB 65ss dentelle at the center front. It also has volcano and crystal copper frames and 3mm bicones in the neckstrap.

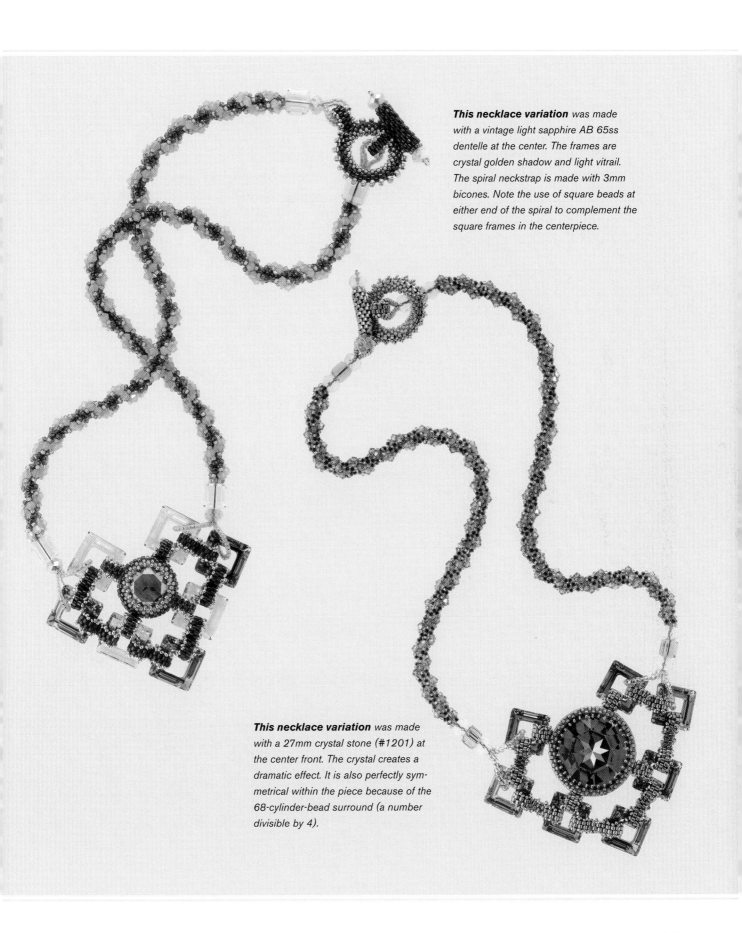

This necklace variation was made with a vintage light sapphire AB 65ss dentelle at the center. The frames are crystal golden shadow and light vitrail. The spiral neckstrap is made with 3mm bicones. Note the use of square beads at either end of the spiral to complement the square frames in the centerpiece.

This necklace variation was made with a 27mm crystal stone (#1201) at the center front. The crystal creates a dramatic effect. It is also perfectly symmetrical within the piece because of the 68-cylinder-bead surround (a number divisible by 4).

LIFE FRAMED BRACELET

Beading time varies, but count on at least 8 to 10 hours

This project was designed for Swarovski Crystal Frames (#4439), a fantastic jewelry component. You'll learn how to interlock components with strips of flat peyote stitch. You will also learn edging and surface-embellishment techniques for flat peyote.

These directions will make a 7" (17.8 cm) bracelet. By adding one more set of two frames, you can add ⁷⁄₈" (2.2 cm) to the length of the bracelet.

To protect the foil backing of your crystal stones, paint it with clear nail polish. There is already a protective finish on the foil, but some people's body chemistry affects the bead finishes. You can apply the polish before you begin or after you finish the bracelet.

MATERIALS

- twelve 14mm square Swarovski frames (#4439), six of color A, six of color B
- 11° Japanese cylinder beads, 10 grams of one color
- 15° Japanese seed beads, 1 gram of one color
- 11° Japanese seed beads, 1 gram of one color
- 15° Czech charlottes, 5 grams of one color
- one 10mm Swarovski margarita (#3700)

TOOLS AND NOTIONS

- size 12 English beading needles
- FireLine, 6 lb. test
- microcrystalline wax
- scissors

Step 1: Making the Connector Strips

Thread half a wingspan of single FireLine. String two cylinder beads, then pick up a third cylinder bead and go back through the first cylinder bead to begin your peyote-stitch strip, which is two beads wide **(a)**.

Continue peyote-stitching back and forth until you have completed forty-eight rows of peyote stitch (count twenty-four beads up each side of the strip).

Ultimately, you will need sixteen peyote-stitch strips in order to link all the crystal frames in the bracelet. As you finish each strip, set it aside. Do not weave in tails, because you'll need them to attach the strip to itself and to add the charlotte edging.

(a)

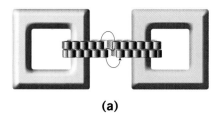

(a)

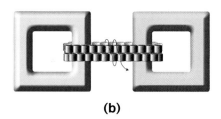

(b)

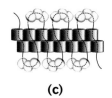

(c)

Step 2: Linking the Crystal Frames

Link frames as follows: pick up one frame in color A and one frame in color B. Hold them wrong sides together. Feed one of the peyote-stitch strips through the holes of both frames. Zigzag through the up beads of the first row of peyote stitch and the last row of peyote stitch on the strip, zipping them together to form a loop that holds both frames, **(a)**.

Lay the frames flat and stitch the top of the connector to the bottom of the connector between the frames to help keep the peyote link flat and the frames separated **(b)**.

Now, working with what is left of your threads, edge the entire link, top side and bottom, using 15° charlottes and zigzagging back and forth from one side to the other, creating alternating picots by coming out of one edge bead, threading three charlottes, and going into the next edge bead **(c)**.

After you have linked one color A frame to one color B frame, repeat this process five more times so you have a total of six sets of linked frames. Now arrange the sets in an alternating manner **(d).**

Link each set to the next, with two connectors, attaching and edging them as you did for the first set. After you have finished, you will have an interlocked piece that is two frames wide and six frames long.

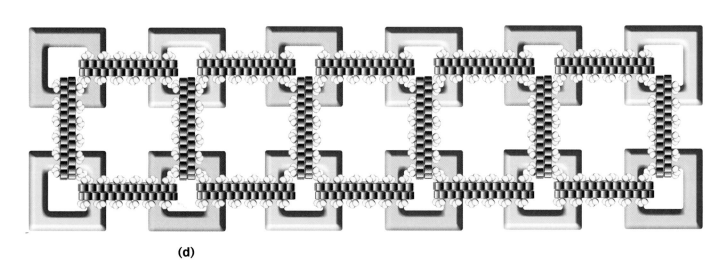

(d)

Step 3: Creating the Button End

Make two peyote-stitch strips, similar to the ones that connect the frames to each other, but two beads wide by thirty-two rows long (sixteen beads up each side of the strip).

Thread one strip through one of the last frames on one end of the bracelet. Working with the tail thread of the strip, zip the strip to itself at the twenty-fourth row. There will be twelve beads along each edge of the "loop" around the frame and a tab coming off of the loop that is eight beads long (four beads up either side of the tab).

Repeat this process with the second peyote strip, threading it through the other frame at this end of the bracelet. When you've finished, this end of the bracelet should look as it does in **(a)**.

Working with the tail thread that is coming out of the first peyote-stitch strip, string fourteen cylinder beads and go through the bottom two beads of the second peyote-stitch strip, as shown **(b)**.

Peyote-stitch back and forth, creating a band that is eighteen beads wide by eighteen rows long (nine beads up each side). Then begin decreasing on both sides of the band by not adding a cylinder bead at the beginning of each row, and instead just going through the next up bead. Continue decreasing in this way until the band tapers off to a point, as shown **(c)**.

Working with the available tail threads or adding a new thread, if necessary, edge the entire band and the two connectors with picots of three charlottes. The straight sides of the band are edged as shown in **(d)**.

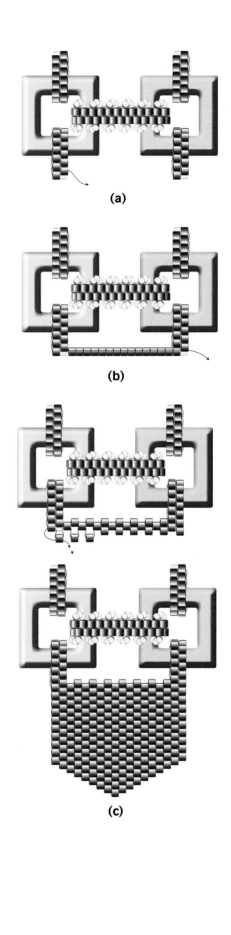

(a)

(b)

(c)

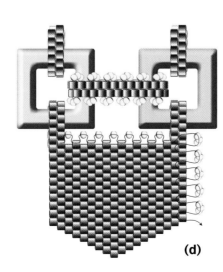

(d)

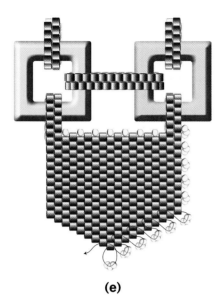

(e)

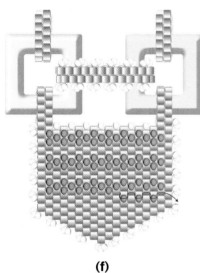

(f)

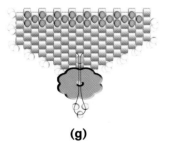

(g)

The diagonal edges of the band are a little more complex to edge, so they will require the threading shown in **(e)**.

After you've completed the edging, add dimension to the closure band by "stitching in the ditch" with 15° seed beads. Beginning in the second row of peyote stitch, come out of one of these second-row cylinder beads, pick up one of the 15°s, and go into the next second-row cylinder bead.

Repeat this technique to embellish the second, third, and fourth rows of cylinders. Then skip over the fifth, sixth, and seventh rows. Begin embellishing again on the eighth, ninth, and tenth rows. Skip over the eleventh, twelfth, and thirteenth rows, and then embellish again on the fourteenth, fifteenth, and sixteenth rows. This sequencing will add an interesting textural design to the closure band **(f)**. ***

When you have finished, stitch on the margarita, which will serve as the button. Weave to the center of the tip of the closure band. Pick up one 11°, which will serve as a button shank. Then pick up the margarita and three 15°s. Go back through the margarita to form a picot of the 15°s. Go back through the 11° and into the band. To reinforce the closure, stitch back up through the 11°, the margarita, and the 15°s and back down again several times **(g)**.

After you've attached the button, knot off and weave in the thread you used to attach the button. Weave in all other tail threads.

Step 4: Creating the Buttonhole End

Create a band in the same way as you did for the button end of the bracelet. Simply follow step 3 to the point marked as ***.

At this point, you will create the button loop. The loop is made by weaving a thread so it comes out of the tip cylinder bead in the triangle end of the band. Coming out of this bead, string twenty-three cylinder beads and then circle back through the tip cylinder bead again to create a circle of beads **(a)**.

Working with 11°s, peyote-stitch around the outside of the cylinder beads, which form the loop of beads **(b)**.

When you get back to the tip cylinder bead, work around the inside of the cylinder beads, peyote-stitching this time with 15°s **(c)**.

To finish off the loop, weave back out to the outermost row (of 11°s), and stitch a picot of three 15° charlottes between each 11° **(d)**. This process will give the outside of the button loop a fancy finish. Knot off and weave in any additional tail threads.

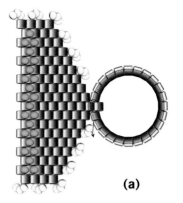

(a)

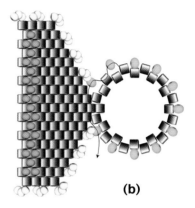

(b)

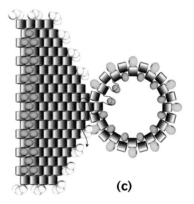

(c)

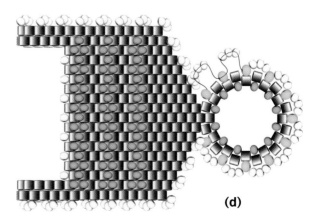

(d)

CRYSTAL FLAT-BACK FLOWER BROOCH

Beading time varies, but count on at least 4 to 6 hours

This project will teach you how to make stunning crystal brooches from flat-back stones. You'll also learn how to bezel on leather.

Step 1: Bezeling the Flat-Back Crystal

Bezel the stone with technique 1 on page 26, then weave your working thread to the back side of the leather. Half-hitch once or twice to secure the thread, then come up through the leather to the top side. Backstitch one additional row of cylinder beads around the perimeter of the bezel. Be sure this row of beads is an even count.

Go back through the beads again to firm up this outer row of embroidery. Go back through the leather to the back side and half-hitch two to three times before cutting off the tail thread.

Step 2: Embellishing the Bezel and Creating the Petals

Next, you'll embellish the bezeled stone. In a real flower, there are often several layers of petals or stamen. You can recreate this effect by layering embellishments and beaded petals.

Work with a double-threaded piece of FireLine so the petals will be firm. Wax it well with microcrystalline wax; it will stick together and function as if it were a single thread.

MATERIALS

- one flat-back crystal stone (round or oval)
- 11° Japanese cylinder beads, 2 grams of one color
- 15° Japanese seed beads, 6 grams total of two or more colors
- 11° Japanese seed beads, 1 gram each of two colors
- 15° Czech charlottes, 1 gram
- 3mm crystal bicones (#5301), quantity will vary depending on size of flat back
- 2mm crystal beads (#5000), quantity will vary depending on size of flat back
- two small scraps of Italian leather, each measuring one inch larger in diameter than the diameter of the flat back
- one base-metal pin back

TOOLS AND NOTIONS

- size 12 English beading needles
- size 12 glover's needles
- FireLine, 6 lb. test
- nylon thread to match the leather
- microcrystalline wax
- scissors
- E6000 adhesive
- toothpicks

(a)

(b)

(c)

To begin, thread 2 yards (1.8 m) of FireLine. Pull the thread through the needle and even up the ends to make a double thread 1 yard (0.9 m) long. Wax well and tie a half-hitch knot at the end of the thread, leaving about a ¼" (6 mm) tail.

Pass the needle through the leather from the back side, coming out between the bezel and the outer row of embroidery. Weave up through the bezel to the topmost row of cylinder beads.

Embellish between every bead in this row with a variation on the crystal burst embellishment (see page 40). Each consists of one 11° seed bead, one 3mm bicone, one 2mm round crystal bead, one 15° seed bead, and one 15° charlotte. Go back down through the 15° seed bead, the 2mm crystal, the 3mm bicone, and the 11°. Go into the next cylinder bead in the row and repeat **(a)**.

When you've completed the first row of embellishment, step down to the row of cylinder beads below. Create a beaded petal between every cylinder bead in this second row. Begin by picking up one 11° and nine 15°s (six of color A and three of color B). Go back through the sixth 15° to form a picot with the last three 15°s (B colored beads). Peyote-stitch back toward the 11° at the base with color A 15°s **(b)**.

When you pick up the last 15°, do a U-turn and come up through the first 15° you strung. Now peyote-stitch around the petal form with 15°s one more time. At the picot tip, pick up one color B and go through the beads in the picot. Pick up one more color B 15° and weave back down to the base **(c)**.

Go through the 11° seed bead at the base of the petal and into the next cylinder bead in the base. Continue all the way around the bezel until there is one petal between every cylinder bead in the row you are working.

When you have finished the petals, weave back down to the base of the bezel and through to the back side of the leather. Half-hitch several times and cut off the tails, leaving a ¼" (6 mm) tail. Set the flower aside.

Step 3: Attaching the Backing

Thread a glover's needle with 36" (91.4 cm) of nylon thread. Wax well and tie a knot, leaving about a ¼" (6 mm) tail. Pass the needle through the leather so you are coming up just inside the outer row of embroidery.

Center the pin back on the leather backing and mark the spots where you need to cut holes for the hook end and hinge end. Cut small holes in the leather with scissors and push the ends of the pin back through the leather to the front side of the backing **(a)**.

With a toothpick, spread an even coating of E6000 adhesive on the back side of the embroidered leather. Place the backing onto the back side of the bezeled-stone leather. Allow the glue to dry for ten to twenty minutes. With sharp, small shears, cut the two pieces of leather, leaving a border of about one bead's width around the outer row of embroidery.

Pass the threaded glover's needle through both layers of leather and flip the flower upside down. Working from the back side, sew the edges of the leather with small, neat stitches, spaced ¹⁄₁₆" to ⅛" (1.6 to 3 mm) apart. When you have finished, pass the needle back up through the leather, coming out just inside the outer row of embroidery on the front.

Sew through a couple of beads in this row and begin peyote-stitching with cylinder beads. Do one row of cylinder beads followed by two rows of 11° seed beads to finish the base row and cover the edges of leather. Half-hitch several times between beads before cutting off the tail thread.

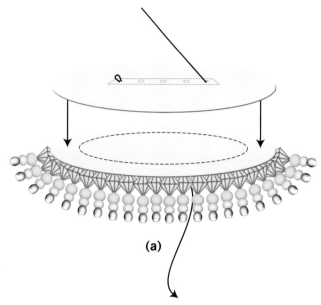

(a)

CRYSTAL DAHLIA NECKLACE

Beading time varies, but count on at least 12 to 16 hours

This clear crystal necklace (shown at right in the photo) is a simplified, crystallized version of a dahlia necklace I made in 2003. The original piece received Best in Show in Bead Dreams 2003 and appeared on the cover of the summer 2004 issue of *Bead & Button Bead Dreams* magazine. It is a wonderful project, inspired by the dahlias I grow in my garden every summer.

Step 1: Bezeling the Crystal Stone

The first step is to bezel the crystal stone that is at the center of the flower. You can choose from a variety of types and sizes, including 14, 16, or 18mm rivolis or 60 or 65ss dentelles (the project uses a 65ss dentelle). Bezel the stone with technique 2 on page 27. Leave the tail threads hanging—you'll need them later to create the bail.

Step 2: Embellishing the Stone and Adding the Petals

Next, embellish the bezeled stone. Just as for Crystal Flat-Back Flower Brooch on page 110, layering embellishments and beaded petals adds dimension to this flower.

Work with a double-threaded piece of FireLine so the petals will be firm and not floppy. Although it is more difficult to work with a double thread, if you wax it well with microcrystalline wax, it will stick together and function as if it were a single thread.

MATERIALS

- 11° Japanese seed beads, 15 grams
- 15° Japanese seed beads, 10 grams each of three colors
- 15° Czech charlottes, 3 grams
- Japanese cylinder beads, 5 grams
- one crystal rivoli or point-backed stone, size can vary
- 3mm or 4mm crystal bicones (#5301), 2–3 gross
- 2mm round crystal beads (#5000), 4–6 gross
- 7mm x 4mm faceted crystal drop beads (#6007), 1–2 gross
- one antique button (for the closure)

TOOLS AND NOTIONS

- size 12 and size 13 English beading needles
- FireLine, 6 lb. test
- microcrystalline wax
- scissors

(a)

(b)

(c)

Thread 2 yards (1.8 m) of FireLine. Pull the thread through the needle and even up the ends, to make a double thread approximately 1 yard (0.9 m) long. Wax well.

Weave up through the bezel to the topmost row of cylinder beads. As with the flower brooch, you will first create a round of embellishment and then a round of petals. Do the same type of first-round embellishment as for the brooch **(a)**. Then weave down to the next row of cylinder beads and do a complete round of petals, with one petal between every cylinder bead in that row. To create beaded petals, follow **(b)**, **(c)**, and the instructions on pages 111–112.

If you still have thread on your needle, leave it for now —you can use it later to add the crystal-bead branch-fringe embellishments behind the petals.

Step 3: Making the Bail

After you've made the petals, you're ready to add the bail. Working with one of the original tails you used when you bezeled the stone, stitch up to the top of the bezel, behind the back row of petals. Now begin a small width (four to six beads wide) of flat peyote stitch, creating a tab that will loop around and attach to create a bail. Make sure the bail is long enough to slide over the spiral-rope neck strap. Embellish both sides of the bail with 15° charlotte picots.

Step 4: Adding the Branch Fringe Embellishments

After you've made the bail, continue embellishing the stone. Work with a double thread for these embellishments to ensure good tension, strength, and overall durability. In the row of cylinder beads directly behind the row in which you made the petals, make a crystal bead branch fringe, following the instructions on page 41. Begin the branch fringes at the top of the stone, where the bail is. Start with a fringe that is three 11°s long.

Moving around the bezel from top to bottom, increase each embellishment by one or two 11°s. When you reach the bottom of the pendant, begin decreasing each embellishment so that it is symmetrical with the first side of embellishments. When you have finished, weave off your thread, half-hitching several times before cutting the tails.

Step 5: Creating the Spiral Neck Strap

The neck strap for this necklace is a crystal spiral rope. You can make any of several variations for this necklace. Refer to the instructions for Crystal Spiral Rope Necklace on page 45. The variation on the project shown here is the same base rope as in Crystal Burst Necklace (see page 79). The core is made from 11°s and the outer beads are as follows: a series of one 15°, one 2mm round crystal bead (article #5000), one 4mm crystal bicone (article #5301), one 2mm round crystal bead (article #5000), and one 15°.

Step 6: Attaching the Clasp

When you've finished the rope, slide the pendant over the spiral before adding the clasp. Choose any of the closures described in chapter six. I chose an antique metal button and the button/spiral taper technique described for the crystal spiral rope on pages 46–47.

Loop closure with antique button

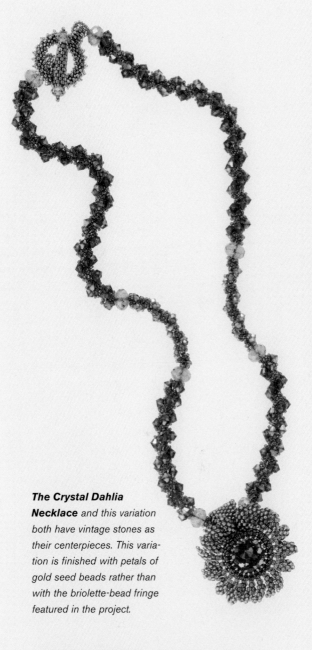

The Crystal Dahlia Necklace and this variation both have vintage stones as their centerpieces. This variation is finished with petals of gold seed beads rather than with the briolette-bead fringe featured in the project.

This necklace features a unique vintage stone, which is flat-topped with a round, faceted, foiled back. Each petal was made with a range of bead sizes, from 11° seed beads (at center) to cylinder beads and then to 15° seed beads along the edge. The varied bead sizes create the curve of the petals. The neck strap is a crystal spiral rope, with occasional spacer beads. The closure is a beaded toggle clasp.

VINEYARD JEWEL NECKLACE

Beading time varies, but count on at least 16 to 20 hours

The sparkling Swarovski rivolis nestled amongst clusters of grapelike pearls reveal my source of inspiration: the vineyards of San Luis Obispo, California. This necklace, along with Rings & Things on page 90, was designed for Beads on the Vine, an annual retreat sponsored by the School of Beadwork and held at the Edna Valley Vineyard in San Luis Obispo.

Step 1: Bezeling the Rivolis

The first step is to bezel the two 18mm rivolis. Bezel these stones with technique 2 on page 27.

Step 2: Making the Suspended Bail

After you have bezeled both of the stones, you are ready to create the suspended bail. This bail is made with Ndebele weave (page 22), which is woven off of the peyote bail in a seamless melding of stitches.

* Working off of the middle row of cylinder beads on the bezeled rivoli, come out of a bead, pick up three cylinder beads, and go back into the next bead in that middle row of cylinder beads **(a)**, next page. Now weave diagonally up to the next cylinder bead, do a U-turn, and come back in the other direction through the cylinder bead directly below the one you just went through, then pass back through the cylinder bead in the middle row.

MATERIALS

- two 18mm Swarovski crystal rivolis (#1122)
- Japanese cylinder beads, 20 grams of one color
- 11° Japanese seed beads, 5 grams each of two colors
- 15° Japanese seed beads, 2 grams each of two colors, 5 grams of a third color
- thirty to forty 4mm Czech fire-polished beads
- thirty 3mm Swarovski crystal bicones (#5301)
- thirty 4mm Swarovski crystal bicones (#5301)
- 15° Czech precious metal charlottes, 4 grams of one color
- one and one-half 16" (40.6 cm) strands 6mm freshwater pearls

TOOLS AND NOTIONS

- size 12 and 13 English beading needles
- FireLine, 6 lb. test
- microcrystalline wax
- scissors

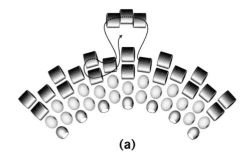

(a)

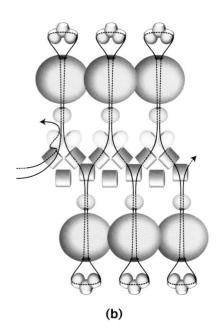

(b)

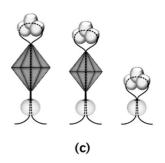

(c)

After coming out of this bead, pick up three more cylinder beads and go back into the original cylinder bead you exited when you began. Do another U-turn to step up into the first of the six cylinder beads you have just added. These six cylinder beads will serve as the basis for a three-ladder tube of Ndebele, which will be built up and away from the bezel.

Working with these six newly added cylinder beads as the base, begin three-ladder tubular Ndebele, following the instructions on page 22. After one round with cylinder beads, step up at the end of the round and do one round with 11° seed beads.

Next begin the pearl embellishments that decorate the suspended bail directly above the bezeled rivoli. Coming out of the first bead in the first ladder of Ndebele, pick up one 11°, one pearl, and three 15° Czech charlottes. For these and subsequent embellishments, use a different color 11° than was used for the core. This will make it much easier to distinguish the core beads from the embellishment beads. Go back through the pearl and the 11° to form a picot of the charlottes, and then back down into the second bead in the first ladder of Ndebele.

Repeat the process between the first and second ladders, then come up in the second ladder and repeat the process a third time. You will have one embellishment on top of and one embellishment between each ladder, for a total of six embellishments on that one row **(b)**.

Now do three rows of Ndebele with 11°s and another row of six-pearl embellishments. Then do two rows of 11°s and one row of 4mm-bicone embellishments in the same way, using 15° seed beads rather than charlottes for the picot on top of each embellishment **(c)**.

Now do another row of 11°s and one row of 3mm bicone embellishments (just as with the 4mm bicones). Do another row of 11°s and one row of simple 11° picot embellishments, done as with the others, but this time with one 11° and then three 15°s to form the picot (see page 39). After you've finished this final row of embellishment, do one more row of 11°s and step up.

Coming out of the first bead of the first ladder, pick up one 4mm Czech fire-polished bead and two 11°s. Go back down through the fire-polished bead and into the second bead on that first ladder of Ndebele. Go up into the first bead of the second ladder and then repeat the 11°/Czech addition (see sidebar).

When you have completed this round, step up through the Czech fire-polished bead and out of the first of the two 11°s that were added on top of the first ladder. You are now ready to begin stitching the next row.

Do three rows of 15°s,** followed by fifteen rows of cylinder beads. Then do three rows of 15°s and one row of 11°s. Add another row of 4mm Czech fire-polished beads (with the two 11°s on top) and three more rows of 15°s.

The final step is to create the bail loop. Working out of the first ladder, pick up two cylinder beads and go back down into the second bead in this first ladder. Do a U-turn and come back up through the first cylinder bead added, and add two more cylinder beads, as shown in the drawing below **(d)**. You have now transitioned into a flat Ndebele only one ladder wide. Continue until you have approximately twenty-six rows.

Zip the last row into one bead on each of the two ladders of Ndebele on the opposite side, splitting the ladders in two. You have now successfully completed the first of the two suspended bails (the pendant that appears on the right-hand side of the necklace in the photo on page 118).

Begin the second, shorter suspended bail as you did the first, beginning at * and ending at **. Now add five rows of cylinder beads and work the bail loop directly out of the top row of cylinder beads.

Go back and add a picot of 15° charlottes to the middle row of cylinder beas both bezels, beginning on one side of the bail and continuing around to the other side, by picking up three beads and going through the next cylinder bead in that middle row.

(d)

THE 11°/CZECH ADDITION

This addition can be a little bit tricky. Begin by coming out the first bead in the first ladder of Ndebele, as if you were going to start a new round.

Pick up one 4mm Czech fire-polished bead, and two more 11°s. Go back down through the 4mm Czech fire-polished bead and go back down into the second bead in the first ladder of Ndebele. Come back up into the first bead in the second ladder of Ndbele and repeat the process.

When you've made this addition on all three ladders, step up through the 11° in the first ladder, then the Czech fire-polished bead and one of the 11°s to get all the way to the top. You're ready to begin again with rows of regular Ndebele with cylinder beads.

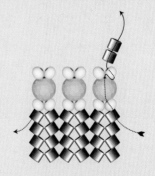

Step 3: Creating the Neck Strap

The neck strap is made with three-ladder tubular Ndebele. Work the stitch according to the instructions on page 22, beginning the initial circle with twelve cylinder beads.

The sequence for the neck strap on the necklace shown in the photograph is as follows:

- 15 rows of cylinder beads

- 3 rows of 15° seed beads

- 1 row of 11° seed beads

- 1 row 11°/Czech fire-polished bead addition (see sidebar, page 121)

- 3 more rows of 15°s

Following this sequence, make five sets, ending the last set with the 11°/Czech fire-polished bead addition.

When you reach the center of the neck strap, you'll apply the same embellishment techniques used in the suspended rivoli pendants. The pattern is as follows:

- 1 row of 11° seed beads

- 1 row of simple 11° picot embellishments on and between each ladder (for a total of 6)

- 1 row of 11° seed beads

- 1 row of 3mm bicone embellishments on and between each ladder (for a total of 6)

- 1 row of 11° seed beads

- 1 row of 4mm bicone embellishments on and between each ladder (for a total of 6)

- 2 rows of 11° seed beads

- 1 row of pearl embellishments on and between each ladder (for a total of 6)

- 3 rows of 11° seed beads

- 1 row of pearl embellishments on and between each ladder (for a total of 6)

- 5 rows of 11° seed beads (slide the finished bail of the second [shorter] pendant over these)

- 1 row of pearl embellishments on and between each ladder (for a total of 6)

- 3 rows of 11° seed beads

- 1 row of pearl embellishments on and between each ladder (for a total of 6)

- 5 rows of 11° seed beads (slide the finished bail of the first [longer] pendant over these)

- 1 row of pearl embellishments on and between each ladder (for a total of 6)

- 3 rows of 11° seed beads

- 1 row of pearl embellishments on and between each ladder (for a total of 6)

- 2 rows of 11° seed beads

- 1 row of 4mm bicone embellishments on and between each ladder (for a total of 6)

- 1 row of 11° seed beads

- 1 row of 3mm bicone embellishments on and between each ladder (for a total of 6)

- 1 row of 11° seed beads

- 1 row of simple 11° picot embellishments on and between each ladder (for a total of 6)

- 1 row of 11° seed beads

- 1 row 11°/Czech fire-polished bead addition

- 3 rows of 15° seed beads

When you have finished this sequence for the center piece, you are ready to continue stitching with cylinder beads. Begin the same sequence you used for the first part of the strap. Make five complete sets, ending with three rows of 15° seed beads.

Step 4: Creating the Button Closure

When you've finished the neck strap (incorporating the pendants along the way), you are ready to make the button closure. This closure consists of a grapelike cluster of pearls at one end and a woven loop at the other.

I usually make the loop on the end that would be in my right hand when I put on the necklace. Because I am right-handed, this positioning makes it easier for me to do up the closure. If you are left-handed, you may want to make the loop on the other end.

Begin by making the button end of the closure. This cluster button mimics the sequence in the centerpiece of the necklace. You ended this side of the strap with three rows of 15° seed beads. Continue with the three-ladder tube of Ndebele as follows:

- 1 row of 11° seed beads
- 1 row 11°/Czech fire-polished bead addition
- 1 row of 11° seed beads
- 1 row of simple 11° picot embellishments on and between each ladder (for a total of 6)
- 1 row of 11° seed beads
- 1 row of 3mm bicone embellishments on and between each ladder (for a total of 6)
- 1 row of 11° seed beads
- 1 row of 4mm bicone embellishments on and between each ladder (for a total of 6)
- 2 rows of 11° seed beads
- 1 row of pearl embellishments on and between each ladder (for a total of 6)
- 3 rows of 11° seed beads
- 1 row of pearl embellishments on and between each ladder (for a total of 6)
- 3 rows of 11° seed beads
- 1 row of pearl embellishments on and between each ladder (for a total of 6)

Begin to taper the end of the button by doing one row of Ndebele in 11°s with only one bead on top of each ladder rather than the usual two. Pass the thread one more time through these three top 11°s to pull the end in tightly. Knot off the thread by half-hitching several times before cutting the tail.

To create the loop end, begin a one-ladder-wide strip of flat Ndebele, as you did for the bail loop. The strip for the loop is made in the following sequence:

- 5 rows of cylinder beads
- 3 rows of 15° seed beads
- 1 row of 15° seed beads/Czech fire-polished bead addition
- 2 rows of 15° seed beads
- 10 rows of cylinder beads
- 1 row of 15° seed beads
- 1 row of 11°s
- 1 row 11°/Czech fire-polished bead addition
- 1 row 15° seed beads
- 10 rows of cylinder beads
- 3 rows of 15° seed beads
- 1 row 15°/Czech fire-polished bead addition
- 2 rows of 15° seed beads
- 5 rows of cylinder beads

Zip the last row back into the two tubes of Ndebele on the side opposite the ladder at the point where you started, as you did with the bail loop.

CROWN JEWELS

Beading time varies, but count on at least 5 to 7 hours

This project was inspired by the sheer magic of crystal and the beauty of mathematics. The cube is a geometric wonder, appearing again and again in many forms within nature. This project will teach you how to make hollow objects that hold their shape without any sort of internal support.

The calculations are exact, so it is important to select stones that have an initial-row count of cylinder beads (for the bezel) that is divisible by four, resulting in an even number. For example, the stone might be encircled by twenty-four, thirty-two, forty, forty-eight, etc., beads. A couple of great choices for this project are:

- 8mm square, #4650 or #4470 (the initial row of cylinder beads is twenty-four beads)

- 13mm crystal rings, #1245 (the initial row of cylinder beads is thirty-two beads)

- 16mm rivoli or 65ss dentelles (the initial row of cylinder beads is forty beads)

MATERIALS
(for one Crown Jewel)

- six crystal stones (in appropriate sizes, as explained at left)
- 11° Japanese cylinder beads, 5 grams of one color
- 15° Japanese seed beads, 4 grams total of two or three colors
- 15° precious metal charlottes, 2 grams
- eighteen 3mm crystal bicones

TOOLS AND NOTIONS

- size 12 English beading needles
- FireLine, 6 lb. test
- microcrystalline wax
- scissors

Step 1: Bezeling the Crystal Stones

The first step is to bezel the six crystal stones. Bezel the stones with technique 2 on page 27. When you have completed each bezel, leave the tail threads—you'll use them to connect the stones.

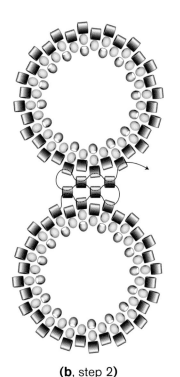

(a, step 2)

Step 2: Forming the Sides

Weave the thread on the first stone down to the middle row of the three rows of cylinder beads at the center of the bezel. Coming out of one of these beads, pick up a cylinder bead and go through the next cylinder bead in the row. The number of cylinder beads you add across will depend on the size of your stones, as follows:

for 16mm rivoli or 65ss dentelle: Add three cylinder beads across and three cylinder beads back (six beads wide).

for 13mm crystal rings: Add two cylinder beads across and two cylinder beads back (four beads wide), as shown in the drawings.

for 8mm square stones: Add one cylinder bead across and one cylinder bead back (two beads wide).

Pick up a bead, and peyote-stitch back the other way so as to create a tab that is two rows long (count one bead up each side). The width will vary depending on stone size, as explained above. You will use this tab to connect one stone to the next **(a)**.

To connect the first bezeled stone, use the tail thread on the tab to zip the first stone to the middle row of cylinder beads on the second stone by zigzagging through the up beads **(b)**.

Then, working with the tail thread on the second rivoli, weave over to the opposite side and position a tab opposite the first one. Repeat to connect the four stones to create the sides of the crystal cube **(c)**.

(b, step 2)

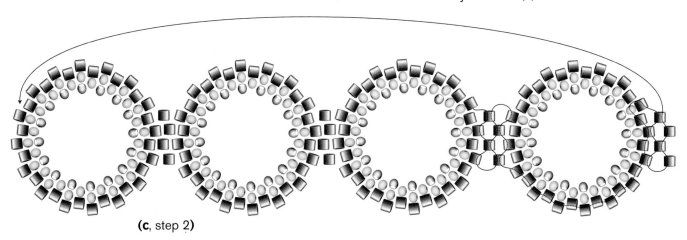

(c, step 2)

After you have zipped the stones to each other, embellish both ends of the tab with three charlottes to form a picot. These picots will form the base from which you will later weave the bicone corners **(d)**.

Step 3: Attaching the Top and Bottom

After you have connected all four sides of the cube, you will make the top and bottom with the last two bezeled stones. Knot off and weave in both tails—you already have plenty of threads to work with.

Working with the cube and leftover tails, weave tabs the same size as the side tabs on the top and bottom of each side stone **(a)**. These tabs should be evenly spaced between the two side-connection tabs.

Attach the top and bottom stones to the sides of the cube by zipping the tabs to each stone's bezel. Again, as before, embellish both ends of the tab with three charlottes **(b)**.

Step 4: Weaving in the Corners

To finish, fill in the corners with 3mm bicones. Weave an available tail up to the charlotte picot on one of the three tabs that encircle the corner hole. Pass through the middle charlotte, pick up two bicones, and go through the next middle charlotte of the next tab picot.

Go back through the second bicone and add a third bicone. Then go through the middle charlotte of the third tab picot. After passing through this charlotte, go back through the third bicone and down through the first bicone. This process will fill in the hole created by joining the rivoli. You may want to pass through the bicones and charlottes a second time, just to reinforce the corner **(a)**.

To create a bead that you can wear on a chain or length of cording—alone or with other beads—leave any two opposite corners open. Simply feed the chain or cording through the two holes to wear the "beaded bead."

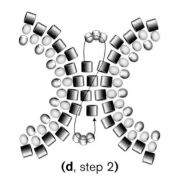

(**d**, step 2)

(**a**, step 3)

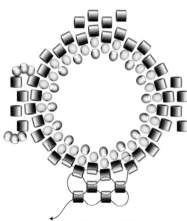

(**b**, step 3)

(**a**, step 4)

VARIATIONS

These crown jewel variations are all made with crystal components. Variations in color and stone size give each one its unique look.

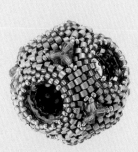

This crown jewel is made with crystal rings (#1245). The initial surround of cylinder beads is made with 32 beads, resulting in a slightly smaller finished crown jewel. A pearl is placed inside the form before the final side is attached. It is strung up at the same time as the bead, to create an inner bead (the pearl) that is separate from the outer bead (the beaded bead) and spins separately.

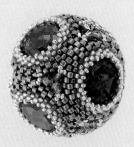

This crown jewel is made with vintage madeira topaz 65ss dentelles. This stone color has not been produced for some time, and is difficult to come by, but there are alternate modern crystal colors.

In this variation, the crystal stones are vintage 65ss light siam AB dentelles. The cylinder beads are delicas that are 24K-plated, producing an almost metallic effect.

This crown jewel was made with very old 55ss crystal dentelles that have a rare "jet iris" finish. The stone size is slightly smaller than the stone size in the project, so you need to reduce the initial row of cylinder beads to a count of 32.

These beads, the smallest of all the crown jewels, are made with vintage 8mm square stones (#4650). Because the stone size is considerably smaller than the size in the project, you need to reduce the count of the initial row of cylinder beads to 24. Although these vintage stones are somewhat difficult to find, Swarovski makes a modern square stone (#4470) that is an excellent substitute and is available in the 8mm size.

This crown jewel is made with antique medium vitrail 65ss dentelles. This vintage color is more golden purple, as opposed to the modern-day, greenish-pink medium-vitrail finish. There are also Aikos and a variety of 15° seed beads. The open corners are filled with 3mm crystal bicones.

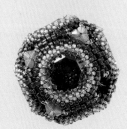

This variation is made with antique 65ss dentelles in light vitrail. The cylinder beads are Toho treasures. There are also a variety of other 15° seed beads. The open corners are filled with 3mm crystal bicones.

This crown jewel is made using vintage starlight 65ss dentelles. The cylinder beads used are Delicas, along with the other 15° seed beads. The open corners are filled with 3mm bicones.

These glass crown jewels are all made with modern Czech glass stones that have been pressed in molds from the Art Nouveau era. The off-centered "volcano cut" adds an air of elegance and asymmetry to this otherwise perfectly geometric form.

This crown jewel variation has light amethyst opal glass stones, in combination with Aikos and a variety of other 15° seed beads. The corners are filled with 3mm bicones.

This crown jewel variation has mustard opal glass stones, Aikos, and assorted 15° seed beads. All but two of the corners are filled with 3mm bicones, to accommodate a chain or neckstrap.

This variation has fuchsia opal glass stones, with Delicas and other 15° seed beads. Six of the eight open corners are filled with 3mm bicones. The other two opposite corners are left open to accommodate a chain or neck strap.

This crown jewel variation has pacific opal glass stones. There are also Aikos and other 15° seed beads. The bead is strung on a length of sheer ribbon, tied at the back of the neck to close.

CRYSTAL GEODESIC DOME

Beading time varies, but count on at least 8 to 10 hours

Like the Crown Jewels, this project was also inspired by mathematics. The dodecahedron (a twelve-sided solid) is an amazing geometric form, based on the Golden Ratio, a mathematical relationship that appears over and over in the natural world.

The calculations are exact, so be sure to select stones that have an initial-row count of cylinder beads (for the bezel) that is divisible by five, resulting in an even number. For example, the stone might be encircled by thirty, forty, fifty, etc., beads. A couple of great choices for this project are:

- 12mm rivoli (the initial row of cylinder beads is thirty beads).

- 16mm rivoli or 65ss dentelles (the initial row of cylinder beads is forty beads).

There are instructions for both sizes.

MATERIALS
(for one Crystal Geodesic Dome)

- twelve crystal stones (in preferred size, as explained at left)
- 11° Japanese cylinder beads, 10 grams of one color
- 15° Japanese seed beads, 8 grams total of two to three colors
- 15° precious metal charlottes, 4 grams
- sixty 3mm crystal bicones

TOOLS AND NOTIONS

- size 12 English beading needles
- FireLine, 6 lb. test
- microcrystalline wax
- scissors

Step 1: Bezeling the Crystal Stones

The first step (regardless of which size you are making) is to bezel the twelve crystal stones. Bezel the stones with technique 2 on page 27. When you have completed each bezel, leave the tail threads—you'll use them to connect the stones.

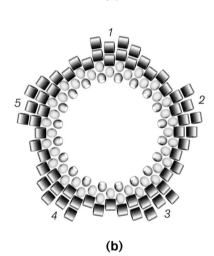

(a)

(b)

Step 2: Adding the Connector Tabs

The next step is to weave the connector tabs. The connector tabs must be spaced exactly and will vary in width, depending on the size of the stone. For the 12mm stone, the connector width will be two beads. For the 16mm stones, the connector width will be four beads, as shown in the drawings.

Weave your tail thread on the first bezeled stone down to the middle row of the three rows of cylinder beads at the center of the bezel. Coming out of one of these beads, pick up a cylinder bead and go through the next cylinder bead in the row **(a)**.

for the 12mm stone: Pick up a bead, and peyote-stitch back the other way to create a tab that is two beads wide by two rows long (count one bead up each side).

for the 16mm stone: Pick up another cylinder bead and go through the next cylinder bead in the base so that you have two cylinder beads that stand out from the bezel. Peyote-stitch back the other way to create a tab that is four beads wide by two rows long (count one bead up each side).

The connector tab will connect one stone to the next. Each bezeled stone will connect to other stones at five points **(b)**.

The spacing between the tabs, regardless of stone size, should be four beads and spaces, as shown in the drawing.

Complete the top and bottom stones first. These are the only two stones that will have five tabs. In the drawings, note how the tabs are at positions 1 through 5. Set aside these two stones.

Now create five more stones, with tabs at positions 3, 4, and 5. Then create five more stones that only have a tab at position 2.

Step 3: Building the Top

You will work with the five stones that have tabs at positions 3, 4, and 5. Attach the stones to form a domed ring by joining the tab at position 5 of one stone to position 2 of the next stone, as shown in **(a)**, **(b)**.

Work all around until the stones are completely joined together. The steps for joining the tab to the next stone are shown in **(c)**.

When you've finished the domed ring, the tabs of the top stone, which you will add later, will fit into position 1 of all the joined stones.

As you build and join tabs to stones, add three-bead picots to both sides of the tab with Czech 15° charlottes. Refer to **(d)** for the exact positioning of the picots.

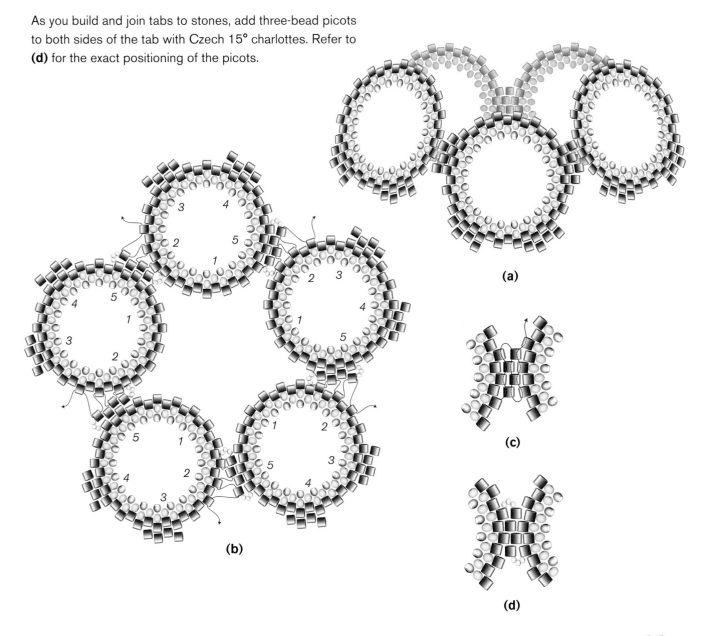

(a)

(b)

(c)

(d)

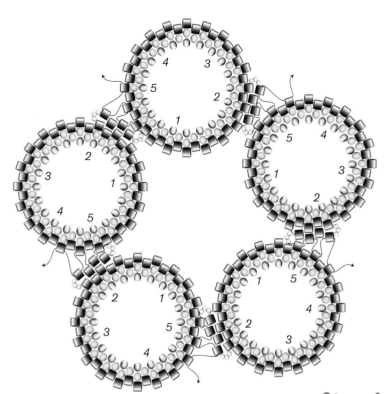

(**a**, step 4)

(**a**, step 6)

Step 4: Building the Bottom

Now you will work the stones that only have a tab in position 2. Attach the stones to form a domed ring, joining the tab at 2 to position 5, as shown in the drawing (**a**). As you did before, picot both ends of the connector tabs.

Step 5: Joining the Top and Bottom

The tabs of the top dome in position 3 and 4 will fit into positions 4 and 3 of the bottom dome. Zip the two domes together at these places to create ten more connector tabs. Again, be sure to picot both ends of each tab after you've joined the domes.

The bottom stones will fit into the openings at position 1 on each of the adjoining stones. Zip this last stone in place.

Step 6: Adding the Bicones

Bicones are added in the same manner as for Crown Jewels. See page 127, step 4, for specifics (**a**).

VARIATIONS

These crystal geodesic domes are all made with crystal stones. One variation can be worn as a pendant. The other two are beaded art objects rather than jewelry pieces.

This 12-sided pendant is made with 12mm cathedral rivolis, cylinder beads, and 15° seed beads. After the stones are bezeled and assembled to form the geodesic dome shape, the corners are filled in with 3mm bicones. The bezels of each of the 12 rivolis are embellished with 11° seed beads added to the top row of cylinder beads to provide a textural element.

This geodesic dome is made with unfoiled, emerald AB, 65ss dentelles, which are set with the point sides out. The bezel is made with Aikos, 15° seed beads, and 15° charlottes. The open corners are filled with 3mm bicones.

This crystal geodesic dome is made with six topaz AB 65ss dentelles and six light sapphire AB 65ss dentelles. The bezel is made with Aikos, 15° seed beads, and 15° charlottes. The open corners are filled with 3mm bicones. After the form was assembled, the bezels of each dentelle were embellished in the top row of cylinder beads with 11° Japanese seed beads. These metallic, plum-colored beads add color and dimension to the form.

INFINITY NECKLACE

Beading time varies, but count on at least 85 to 100 hours.

This necklace is an elaboration of the geometric beadwork techniques used in Crown Jewels. Multiple Crown Jewel beads are linked together with spiral rope, which is then embellished with brange fringe. The centerpiece is a bead within a bead.

Step 1: Creating the Four Large Beaded Beads

The first step is to build the four large beaded beads that will be incorporated into the finished piece. Follow the instructions for Crown Jewels on pages 125–127 to make these beaded beads.

Step 2: Creating the Three Small Beaded Beads

Build three smaller beaded beads on the same principle as the larger beads, but with either 8mm square crystal stones (#4650) or 13mm crystal rings (#1245). The only difference is in the counts needed to encircle and bezel the stones or rings. The chart on page 142 provides the counts for round and square stones and rings.

After you've bezeled the stones, assemble them into beaded beads, as you did the large stones in step 1. Place a 6mm pearl inside the form before adding the sixth side. Be sure to leave two opposite corners open, so you will be able to string the beads later.

Set two of the small beaded beads aside for the back portion of the necklace. You'll incorporate the third bead in the centerpiece, to make a beaded bead within an open-frame beaded bead—the Ultimate Beaded Bead.

MATERIALS

- twenty-four dentelles or crystal stones (65ss, or 16mm)
- twelve 6mm or 8mm crystal rondelles (#5040)
- twenty-two 6mm or 8mm freshwater pearls
- 11° Japanese cylinder beads, 15 grams each of three colors
- 11° Japanese seed beads, 40 grams
- 15° Japanese seed beads, 10 grams each of three colors
- 15° Czech charlottes, 15 grams
- 3 mm crystal bicones (#5301), 160 beads (for corners of beaded beads), 4 gross for fringe
- 4 mm crystal bicones (#5301), 18 beads (for corners of center open framed bead)
- eighteen 13mm crystal rings

TOOLS AND NOTIONS

- sizes 12 and 13 English beading needles, size 12 long English beading needle
- FireLine, 6 lb. test
- microcrystalline wax
- scissors

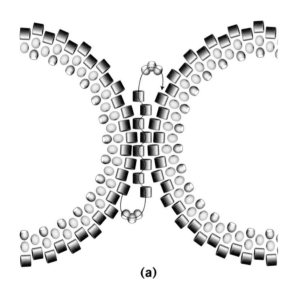

(a)

Step 3: The Ultimate Beaded Bead

You already made the inner bead for the centerpiece in step 2. Now you'll create the open-frame outer bead that contains the small, inner bead.

The outer bead is made up of six bead rings, which are attached to form a cube shape. These rings can be one of two different sizes, depending on how large you want the final bead. Rings may have a circumference of fifty-six cylinder beads or sixty-four cylinder beads. The number of cylinder beads must always be divisible by four, resulting in an even number.

If your inner bead is made with 8mm stones, I suggest making rings with a circumference of fifty-six cylinder beads. If your inner bead is made with crystal rings, I suggest making rings with a circumference of sixty-four cylinder beads. To make the beaded rings, follow the directions for the round toggle closure on page 35.

To attach one ring to the next, weave out of the middle row of cylinder beads on the first ring. Create a tab of even-count flat peyote stitch that is two rows long and eight beads wide (for a fifty-six-bead ring), as shown in the drawing, or ten beads wide (for a sixty-four-bead ring). When you've completed the tab, zip it to the next ring by zigzagging through the up beads. After you've attached the rings, picot both ends of the connector tab, as shown in the drawing **(a)**. This picot will serve later as the base from which the crystal corners are attached.

Continue zipping one ring to the next until you have four rings zipped together to form a square (a "box" of sorts, with no top or bottom), just as you did when you made the Crown Jewels (see page 126).

Now you need to attach the top and bottom to your cube. Weave the tails that you used to attach the connector tabs to the adjacent rings up to the top side of each ring. Build connector tabs on top of each ring—these should be eight or ten beads wide by two rows long. When positioning these top tabs, be sure there are six spaces and beads (a space, a bead, a space, a bead, a space, a bead) on the ring's middle row of cylinder beads between each tab.

Working with these four connector tabs, zip the top ring into place on top of the four sides of the cube. After you've made this connection and picoted the ends of each tab, weave in the 4mm bicones to fill in the corners of the beaded bead **(b)**. Follow the instructions on page 127 to add the bicones in the corners. Be sure to leave two opposite corners of the cube free of bicones so you can string the bead through the two openings.

Before attaching the bottom of the outer bead, place the inner bead within the outer bead. Then attach the last ring. The small bead will now be free-floating inside the large bead. Weave in all threads, half-hitching a couple of times before cutting the tails.

(b)

Step 4: Creating the Toggle Closure

The toggle clasp at the back of this necklace is made entirely of peyote-stitched beads. There is no internal support. Follow the instructions on page 35 to make the toggle clasp.

Step 5: Linking All of the Components Together

Now you are ready to begin assembling all the parts. The parts and pieces of this necklace are linked together with a continuous spiral, which incorporates the beaded beads. Then, if you wish, you can embellish the spiral with branch fringe, as I did for the project shown in the photograph.

Step 6: Creating the Spiral Rope

Begin your spiral as usual (see page 45). Be sure to use a lot of thread, as spiral is a very thread-hungry stitch. If you begin with two to three wingspans of thread, you won't have to constantly start new threads.

As with the Crystal Spiral Rope Necklace on page 45, use 11° seed beads for your core beads and an outer sequence of two 15°s, one cylinder, and two more 15°s. When you've created a section of spiral that is between 1" and 2" long (2.5 and 5.1 cm), you are ready to incorporate the first beaded bead.

Step 7: Incorporating the Beaded Beads

Using the long needle, thread a pearl, a sequence of three 11°s, one 4mm bicone, go through the contained pearl, thread one 4mm bicone, and three 11°s. This strand should extend from one side to the other on the inside of the small beaded bead. Then pick up another pearl, three 11°s (core-bead color), and two 15°s, a cylinder bead, and two more 15°s (outer-sequence color). Go back down through the pearl, through the strand inside the beaded bead, through the first pearl, and down through three core beads in the original section of the spiral rope **(a)**.

Pick up two 15°s, a cylinder bead, and one 15° (outer-sequence color), and go back through the pearl, the strand inside the beaded bead, the second pearl, and two core beads in the new section of spiral rope. Pick up two 15°s and one cylinder bead (outer-sequence color), and go back down through the pearl, through the strand inside the beaded bead, through the first pearl, and down through two core beads in the original section of spiral rope **(b)**.

Now pick up two 15°s and one cylinder bead (outer-sequence color), and go back through the pearl, through the strand inside the beaded bead, the second pearl, and one core bead in the new section of spiral rope. Pick up two 15°s (outer-sequence color), and go back down through the pearl, through the strand inside the beaded bead, through the first pearl, and down through one core bead in the original section of spiral rope **(c)**.

Now pick up two 15°s (outer-sequence color), and go back through the pearl, through the strand inside the beaded bead, the second pearl, and all three core beads in the new section of spiral rope. Pick up one 11° (core-bead color), and two 15°s, one cylinder bead, and two more 15°s (outer-sequence colors) and resume spiral rope stitch in this second section **(d)**.

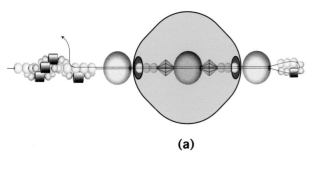

(a)

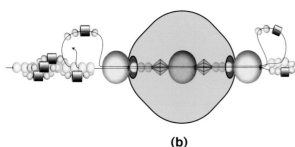

(b)

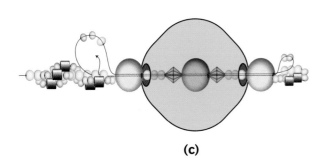

(c)

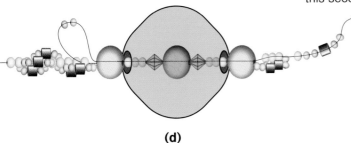

(d)

When this second section of rope is the desired length, you will add a spacer sequence, and then make a third section of rope. The spacer sequence consists of one rondelle, one small tubular bead made of cylinder beads, and one more rondelle.

To make the tubular bead, peyote-stitch a strip of cylinder beads that is four beads wide and fourteen rows long (count seven beads along the sides). Zip the first row to the last by zigzagging through the up beads. After you've made this connection, add a third section of spiral rope, one pearl, a sequence of 11°s that reaches from one side of the large beaded bead to the other, the large beaded bead, one pearl, etc.

When you get to the centerpiece (the Ultimate Beaded Bead), thread large beads between the inside corner of the outside bead and the outside corner of the inside bead. The necklace shown here has two 11°s and one rondelle on each side of the inside bead. This sequence ensures that the inner bead stays evenly centered within the outside, open-frame bead.

Step 8: Adding the Toggle Closure

Working with the thread at the end of the spiral rope, pick up one "end bead" (a pearl). Thread seventeen to twenty-one 15°s (depending on how many will fit through the connection loop on the clasp). Now slide the toggle (loop or bar) up and over the 15°s.

Come back down through the end bead and through three of the core beads in the spiral rope. Pick up two 15°s, one cylinder, and one 15° (outer color sequence). Go back up through the end bead and through the 15°s to help reinforce the clasp attachment.

Now go back down through the end bead again and, this time, go down through two of the core beads in the spiral rope. Pick up two 15°s and one cylinder bead and go back up through the end bead and through the 15°s (with the toggle on them) again, to help reinforce the clasp attachment. Repeat this process, going through one core bead and picking up two 15°s. These actions taper the end of the rope for an attractive, finished look. (For more on tapering, see pages 46–47.)

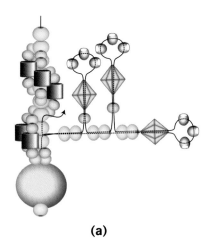

(a)

Step 9: Embellishing with Branch Fringe

If you wish, you can add branch fringe to the spiral rope between beaded beads. The branch fringe will thicken the appearance of the spiral, giving the necklace a more massive, dramatic look.

When making branch fringe, I recommend working with a double thread. By creating a branch between every core bead in the sections of spiral with double thread, you will create a branch embellished crystal bicones **(a)**. See the drawing at left and refer to page 41 for instruction.

Guidelines for Bezeling Crystal Stones and Rings

Article # and shape	Size (mm)	Cylinder beads in initial circle	Back side	Front side	Width of connector tab
4650 DENTELLE OR OTHER ROUND STONE	16mm or 65ss	40 cylinder beads	2 rows 15° 1 row charlottes	3 rows 15° 1 row charlottes	6 beads wide
4650 SQUARE STONE	8mm	24 cylinder beads	1 rows 15° 1 row charlottes	1 rows 15° 1 row charlottes	2 beads wide
1245 CRYSTAL RING	13mm	32 cylinder beads	1 rows 15° 1 row charlottes	3 rows 15° 1 row charlottes	4 beads wide

Vintage to Modern Swarovski Conversion Chart

Description	Vintage article #	Possible modern substitutes
RIVOLI	1122	1122 still available
DENTELLE, 60ss	1200	1200 still available in 60ss
DENTELLE, 65ss	1200	No longer available in 65ss, but a 16mm rivoli will work
SQUARE STONE	4650, 4652	4461 or 4470
LARGE ROUND STONE	1201 (27mm)	1201 still available

Stone Size to Millimeter Conversion Chart*

Stone size	Diameter	Stone size	Diameter
38ss	7.9–8.2mm	47ss	10.5–10.9mm
39ss	8.2–8.4mm	48ss	10.9–11.3mm
40ss	8.4–8.7mm	49ss	11.3–11.7mm
41ss	8.7–8.9mm	50ss	11.7–11.9mm
42ss	8.9–9.2mm	55ss	12.9–13.2mm
43ss	9.2–9.5mm	60ss	14.2–14.5mm
44ss	9.5–9.8mm	65ss	15.5–15.7mm
45ss	9.8–10.2mm	70ss	16.7–16.9mm
46ss	10.2–10.5mm	75ss	17.9–18.2mm

*NOTE: Stone sizes 37 or less are too small for the projects in this book. For that reason, you will find conversions only for the available stone size from 38 up.

SOURCES OF SUPPLY

The materials used in this book are both vintage and modern. In an attempt to assist you in locating the materials used in each project, I have posted an online appendix that details each project's materials in terms of beads and stones used and the manufacturer's color and style identification numbers for these items. You can find this appendix and other book-related support online at www.creativepub.com or www.creatingcrystaljewelry.com.

All of the seed beads are Japanese or Czech, and are, at the time of this writing, of modern manufacture and readily available in the U.S. market. To locate these beads, check with your local bead store or search online.

Crystal materials can present a greater challenge. Vintage items are becoming more difficult to come by because of an increase in demand in the past few years. Specialists in vintage crystals beads and stones can be found online in cases where local bead stores do not

stock historic items. I have also, where applicable, noted the modern Swarovski stone equivalents to the vintage items used. These modern pieces will be much easier to locate and provide an excellent substitute.

Basic supplies, including needles, wax, threads, bead boards, pliers, etc., are usually available at local bead stores and can also be located online.

Just Let Me Bead will be providing a limited number of materials kits for several of the projects contained in this book. These kits will provide all the necessary materials to complete the specified project and will be available for order online at www.justletmebead.com.

For more information on Swarovski products and Swarovski's DIY (do it yourself) Division, please visit the official Swarovski website at www.swarovski.com or http://www.create-your-style.com/website.php.